Starters & Afters

GW01417860

£1-50

Starters & Afters

Over 100 Recipes for
First and Last Courses

Anne Mason

David & Charles: Newton Abbot

0 7153 6343 3

© Anne Mason 1974

Set in 11 on 13pt Bembo
and printed in Great Britain
by Latimer Trend & Company Ltd Plymouth
for David & Charles (Holdings) Limited
South Devon House Newton Abbot Devon

Contents

CONTENTS

List of Plates

Planning Your Menus Ahead

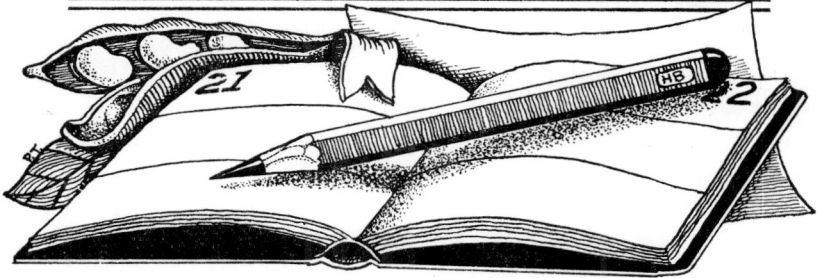

Gone are the days when every dinner was a performance, with a multiplicity of courses following in procession from a well-staffed kitchen.

Today's usual three courses all too often come from a servantless kitchen where the 'lady of the house' is also the 'chief cook and bottle-washer', but when she has guests she can welcome them to her table without fuss and bother because she has planned the meal carefully beforehand, and knows it is well balanced and well cooked.

Family meals, too, can be well planned, and many women find that to work out menus for a week at a time saves trouble and waste, and makes shopping simpler.

Others prefer to work on a day to day basis, building the menu round the best buys in the shops. This is particularly so for women who work outside their homes and do their shopping each day.

But when guests have been asked for dinner it is essential to sit down with paper and pencil and work out the menu well ahead of time. The hostess-cook must take into consideration the tastes of her guests, the amounts necessary to feed the number invited, and what foods are seasonable and at their best at the time.

If she has help in the kitchen there can be a wider choice of dishes, but the single-handed cook who is also the hostess should not choose dishes which will spoil if kept cooking because a guest is late, or which need a lot of last-minute fixing before serving.

If *you* want to enjoy your own party and the dinner you have cooked, plan the dishes so that you can sit down with your guests without having to rush to the kitchen at frequent intervals to see how everything is doing.

Three courses is quite enough for dinner, and all that most people expect. Decide on the main course first, then choose suitable dishes for the beginning and ending, for those first impressions of a meal are important, just as the last course should be one to remember happily as guests leave the table.

Plan the meal to make it easier for yourself. Many appetising dishes can be prepared ahead of time, and those of you who have home freezers will know the dishes which can be made up weeks ahead and frozen, then taken out ready to be heated up and served. A cold first course that can be set on the table before the guests arrive is often more convenient than a hot dish which needs last-minute cooking and serving. The exception to this is hot soup, which looks nicer and keeps hotter if put into a tureen in the kitchen and then served at table.

Contrast is the main aim when planning a dinner. It would be very unwise to serve a thick soup such as minestrone and then follow it with a stew or casserole. Similarly you would not serve a Sole Mornay before a Blanquette de Veau—because both are covered with a rich white sauce.

The same rule applies to the last course, which can be either a savoury or a sweet. For instance, when starting a meal with melon cocktail you would not finish with a fruit salad; or if the main course was served with a cheese sauce you would not serve a Welsh Rarebit to finish the dinner.

Good balance in a meal is important, just as its appearance helps to make it appetising. These days, when so many people are watching their calories, rich, heavy meals are not usually favoured. Dishes should be uncomplicated, easy to digest and served in fairly modest helpings.

If you serve lots of bits and pieces with pre-dinner drinks don't serve hors-d'oeuvre to start the meal. I think that only very simple things like peanuts or olives or tiny cheese biscuits are necessary with drinks before a meal, but that is a matter of choice.

Don't always think you have to serve expensive foods to make a good dinner party—there are many dishes which are just as acceptable and frequently more tasty which can be made with quite humble foods. You may need to take a little more time perhaps, to garnish them with a little more care, but that is well worth it for the end product.

You will find kipper pâté just as tasty as pâté de foie gras (personally, I prefer it), and a colourful platter of crudités not only looks attractive but offers good texture and taste contrast at reasonable cost.

And remember, a good tasty casserole made with a cheaper cut of meat and cooked slowly until tender is much more acceptable than a tough duck, no matter how elegant it looks.

The wise housewife will also take advantage of the convenience foods which are available to help make her job of catering for family and friends easier and more variable. I don't mean she should make packaged and canned foods the steady diet for her family, but there are occasions when a packaged sauce, canned mushrooms or bought puff pastry can save not only time but a lot of worry and energy.

Technology has done so much to make these foods not only convenient but palatable, and your skill as a cook can do more by adding the little extra seasonings, the pat of butter or the dash of wine which can transform them into gourmet items.

Every family probably has its favourite convenience foods which are kept in stock. Two I find invaluable are packaged chocolate pudding and dried onion flakes—the latter because I hate to peel and chop just a small piece of onion for a recipe, then find that the remainder goes mouldy, whereas a few dried flakes do the job just as well. And the chocolate pudding can be used as the filling for a pastry case or sponge flan, served over sponge squares, or poured over fruit—and my young grandsons demand it every time they come for a meal.

Your family favourites may be instant mashed potato or bottled mayonnaise, packaged cake mixes or ready-made meringues, but whatever you find convenient make sure you have supplies in your cupboard for future occasions. As my grandmother always told me, never refuse a helping hand, and in this case, a helping package.

Measurements & Temperatures

Although metrication has finally caught up with us it will probably be many years before today's housewife discards her old kitchen scales and favourite measuring cup and spoon, but tomorrow's housewives—the ones who are today learning to cook metrically at school—will take it as a normal procedure. For them I give all the recipes that follow in both old and new measures, using 25g as the basic unit as advised by the United Kingdom Federation for Education in Home Economics, although this will give a very slightly smaller finished product than the old measurements.

Measurements as used throughout the USA are also given, and it should be noted that the American pint is 16 fl oz as compared to the British Imperial pint of 20 fl oz. American housewives use a standard 8oz or ½ pint cup, whereas British housewives use a BSI cup of 10oz or ½ Imperial pint.

In Australia the Imperial pint of 20 fl oz is used, but their standard cup is 8oz, or the same as the American.

Comparing the Imperial and American standard tablespoon there is

so little difference that I have used the same standard spoons in measurements all through this book. All spoon measurements are level unless otherwise stated.
The following tables may be helpful.

SOLID MEASUREMENTS

British measure		USA equivalent
1oz	flour	¼ cup
4oz		1 cup
1lb		4 cups
4½oz	icing sugar (sifted confectioner's sugar)	1 cup
4oz	castor or granulated sugar	¼ cup
8oz		1 cup
1lb		2 cups
½oz	butter or margarine (shortening)	1 tbsp
8oz		1 cup
1lb		2 cups
2oz	fresh breadcrumbs or cake crumbs	1 cup
4oz	grated cheese	1 cup
4oz	chopped nuts	1 cup
5–6oz	currants, sultanas, raisins	1 cup
4oz	ground almonds	1 cup
1oz	chocolate	1 square

LIQUID MEASUREMENTS

USA	Imperial	Metric
2 tbsp	2 tbsp; 1 fl oz	28ml
¼ cup	4 tbsp; 2 fl oz	56ml
½ cup; ¼ pint	8 tbsp; 4 fl oz	113ml
generous ½ cup	¼ pint; 5 fl oz	142ml
¾ cup	6 fl oz	170ml
1 cup; ½ pint	8 fl oz	226ml
1¼ cups	½ pint; 10 fl oz	284ml

14

1½ cups	12 fl oz	339ml
2 cups; 1 pint	16 fl oz	454ml
2½ cups	1 pint; 20 fl oz	568ml, generous ½l
3¾ cups	1½ pints; 30 fl oz	852ml
4 cups; 2 pints	32 fl oz	908ml
5 cups	2 pints; 40 fl oz (1 quart)	1·14l

OVEN TEMPERATURES

The following table gives the conversions from degrees Fahrenheit to degrees Celsius (formerly called Centigrade) as used for electric cookers, and also numbers used for gas cookers. This is an approximate guide only, as different makes of cookers can vary. If in any doubt refer to the manufacturer's chart which should be supplied with your cooker. The heat is in centre of oven.

Heat of oven	°F	°C	Gas Mark
Very slow	225	110	¼
	250	130	½
	275	140	1
Slow	300	150	2
	325	160	3
Moderate	350	180	4
	375	190	5
Moderately hot	400	200	6
	425	220	7
Hot	450	230	8
Very hot	475	240	9

DIFFERENCES IN COOKING TERMS

British	USA
plain flour	all-purpose flour
cornflour	cornstarch
any fat such as butter or margarine	shortening
treacle	substitute molasses
walnuts	substitute pecans

wholemeal flour	*substitute* **Graham flour**
wholemeal or digestive	
biscuits	*substitute* **Graham crackers**
sweet biscuits	*cookies*
plain dry biscuits	*crackers*
scones	*biscuits*
jelly	*Jello*
jam	*jelly*
tarts or flans	*pies*
pies	*deep-dish pies*
icing sugar	*confectioner's sugar*
sultanas	*seedless raisins*
raisins	*seeded raisins*
melted butter	*drawn butter*
bicarbonate of soda	*baking soda*
single cream	*light cream*
whipping or double cream	*heavy cream*
frying pan	*skillet*
icing (for cakes)	*frosting*

Part 1. Starters

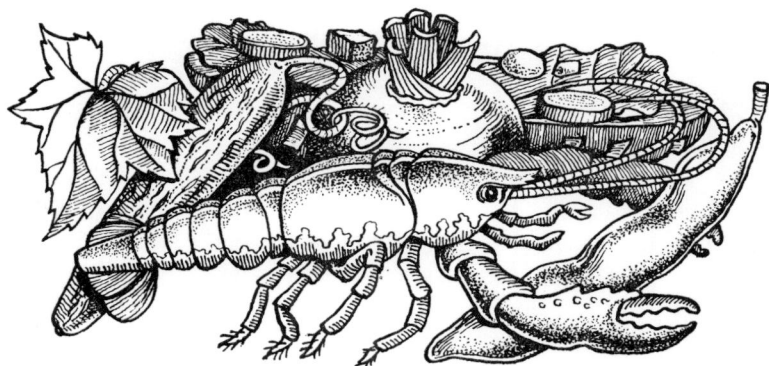

Hors-d'oeuvre

The term hors-d'oeuvre is sometimes frightening to many housewives planning a dinner party who have visions of the very complicated and usually expensive dishes served in so many restaurants under that title. Or they remember the well-laden trolleys of sometimes rather tired-looking 'bits and pieces' brought round to the table in those same restaurants.

But for a home dinner party the 'beginnings' or first course should be simple and at the same time appetising, as those familiar with meals in Continental homes will know.

Think of the French plat de crudités, which usually consists of a platter of whatever fresh vegetables are in season. You can choose from crisp radishes, thinly sliced sticks of celery, grated raw carrots, sliced tomatoes and cucumbers sprinkled with finely chopped parsley or chives, tiny flowerets of cauliflower, all arranged with an eye for colour and design, and served with a simple oil and vinegar dressing or a rich mayonnaise as you please.

Or the Italian antipasto misto, which is usually a platter of thinly sliced salami and mortadella sausages, black or green olives, a few anchovies, sometimes a mound of white haricot beans in oil and vinegar dressing or some crisp fresh radishes, all—like the crudités—arranged with an eye for colour and texture.

Hors-d'oeuvre and canapés (these latter are the ones you serve with drinks before coming to the table for dinner) are not a new invention of modern hostesses, for records show that as early as 300 BC appetisers were served at elaborate parties in Greece. These included a variety of olives, spicy cheeses, roasted nuts and pickled fish—not so different from today's appetisers.

Rich gourmets in Rome spent amazing sums on meals to entertain their friends, and it was quite usual to serve some fifty different kinds of appetisers at a formal dinner, ranging from eel roe, eaten as caviar would be today, to peacocks' tongues and the eggs of exotic birds.

But today's hostesses need not worry about such extravagances, for the choice of foods available is so wide that all tastes are catered for at prices to suit. But always keep in mind that the first course is only served as the prelude to a much more substantial main dish, so make the beginning of the meal look attractive and tempting as an indication that better things are still to come.

Almost every country serves appetisers, although by different names, and for those who enjoy foreign menus here is a list of those names.

Dutch	Voorgerechten
French	Hors-d'oeuvre
German	Vorspeisen
Greek	Mezedakia
Italian	Antipasto
Portuguese	Acepipes
Russian	Zukuska
Spanish	Entremeses
Turkish	Mezeler

Hors-d'oeuvre Variés

These are a collection of simple dishes set out for guests to help themselves at the table, or they are ideal for a buffet dinner party.

For a dinner party of, say, eight people, the different hors-d'oeuvre look attractive and very appetising if set out on matching plates arranged on a large tray, which makes them easier to serve. Or a selection of different foods can be carefully arranged on individual plates, giving attention to the various colours and textures.

Some suggestions include:

Egg Mayonnaise made with required number of hard boiled eggs cut into quarters, then covered with mayonnaise (*p* 119) to which you have added finely chopped parsley or chives.

Orange Vinaigrette made by carefully peeling 4 to 6 oranges, slicing them crosswise on to a dish, then sprinkling with chopped chives. Cover with sauce vinaigrette (*p* 122) at least 30 min before serving.

Grated Raw Carrots marinated for 15 min in sauce vinaigrette. Chopped chives can be added if available.

Tomato and Cucumber Slices arranged alternately in rows, sprinkled with finely chopped spring onions and dressed with sauce vinaigrette or mayonnaise.

Creamy Sweetcorn easily made with an 11½oz (285g) can of sweetcorn with peppers mixed with 2 or 3 tbsp sour cream. Turn out on a serving dish and sprinkle with paprika.

Sardines and Pickled Cucumber: Drain oil from large can of sardines into a bowl. Cut tails from fish and arrange flat in a serving dish. To the oil add salt, pepper, pinch sugar and 2 tbsp (28ml) vinegar (use vinegar from pickled cucumber if available) and mix well, then pour over fish. Chop pickled cucumber and sprinkle over fish.

Dressed Butter Beans: These must be prepared some hours before serving. Drain a large can of butter beans into a bowl. Add either finely chopped onion or chopped chives, also chopped canned pimento and 2 or 3 tbsp French dressing (*p* 122), and mix well. Leave for some hours until ready to serve. Broad beans, either freshly cooked or canned, are also good prepared like this.

Tomato and Anchovies easily made by peeling and slicing ripe tomatoes into a serving dish, then sprinkling them with well-drained chopped anchovies. Season well with pepper.

Stuffed Pepper Slices: These can be made with either red or green peppers, or a mixture of both. Cut slice from stem end of each pepper, carefully remove all seeds and pith. Blend cream cheese with finely chopped celery, adding a little mayonnaise (*p* 119) if necessary, then fill peppers with mixture. Chill until firm, then cut in slices and add to hors-d'oeuvre tray.

Sweet-Sour Apple and Celery made with 2 large cooking apples such as Granny Smith, ½ Spanish onion, crisp celery hearts and French dressing (*p* 122). Peel and core apples and cut into ½in thick strips. Cut celery into same-size pieces—there should be the same amount of celery as apple strips. Mix with onion and toss in French dressing. Chill and serve with hors-d'oeuvre tray.

Sliced salami, krakauer or garlic sausages and mixed green and black olives are good additions to these mixed appetisers. On other pages there are a number of recipes for dishes which can be added to the hors-d'oeuvre tray as desired.

Ham and Asparagus Rolls (serves 8)

8 thin slices pressed cooked ham	*canned pimento*
32 asparagus spears, canned or	*lettuce*
freshly cooked	*mayonnaise (p* 119)

Cut each slice of ham in halves. Cut pimento into 16 strips. Place 2 spears of asparagus on each ½ slice ham and roll up firmly. Wrap a strip of pimento round each roll and fasten with cocktail sticks if necessary. Place 2 rolls on a crisp lettuce leaf for each serving. Hand round mayonnaise separately.

Sliced tomatoes or hard boiled eggs can be used to garnish these if desired.

Peperonata (serves 6)

A well-known Italian dish which is best eaten hot as a first course. If you have any left over it heats up well the next day, or it can be served cold.

8 ripe red peppers	*1 crushed clove of garlic*
10 large ripe tomatoes	*butter or oil*
1 large onion, sliced	*salt and pepper to taste*

Halve peppers and remove seeds and pith, then cut in strips. Peel and slice tomatoes. Brown onion and garlic in butter or oil (or a mixture of both) for 10 min. Add pepper strips, cover and cook for 15 min, then add tomatoes and cook for another 20 min, stirring occasionally. The mixture should be fairly dry and a tasty amalgam of all the vegetables.

A dozen black olives can be added for the last 5 min of cooking time, and some recipes add grated cheese at the end, but this is a matter of taste.

Leeks à la Grecque

This is an unusual appetiser which has a very good flavour, and can be prepared in the morning and left to chill until ready to serve. Celery hearts cut into quarters can be cooked and served in the same way.

	USA	Imperial	Metric
water	2¼ cups	1 pint	568ml
lemon juice	2 tbsp	2 tbsp	28ml
olive oil	2 tbsp	2 tbsp	28ml
bay leaf	1	1	1
thyme and parsley, a few sprigs			
celery	1 stick	1 stick	1 stick
salt	¼ tsp	¼ tsp	¼ tsp
peppercorns	4–5	4–5	4–5
leeks, as required			
parsley, finely chopped, to taste			

Put water, lemon juice, olive oil, bay leaf, thyme, parsley, celery, salt and peppercorns into a saucepan and boil for 5 min. Strain and put back into saucepan.

Cut white part of leeks into 3in lengths and wash very well. Add to above liquid and boil gently until leeks are tender but unbroken. Cool in liquor, then drain and chill until ready to serve; sprinkle with finely chopped parsley.

Ratatouille Niçoise (serves 6)

This is a famous and very popular dish from Provence, and particularly from the very attractive city of Nice. There are many different versions of this recipe, which is usually served hot as a first course, but is equally good when served cold. It takes about 1 hr of slow cooking, and if I think dinner might be delayed I turn the cooked mixture into a fairly shallow brown ovenproof pottery casserole with a good fitting lid and keep it hot in a very slow oven (275° F, 140° C, Gas Mark ½), but I would not advise keeping it hot like this for more than 20 min. I serve it at the table from the casserole into small brown pottery dishes.

		USA	Imperial	Metric
olive oil		4 tbsp	4 tbsp	56ml
medium onions		2	2	2
green peppers		2	2	2
aubergines		2–3	2–3	2–3
courgettes		1lb	1lb	400g
tomatoes		1lb	1lb	400g
salt and pepper, to taste				
garlic		2 cloves	2 cloves	2 cloves
parsley, to taste				

Peel the aubergines and cut into finger-size pieces. Scrub the courgettes, cut off each end and then cut into pieces about the same size as the aubergines. Put into a bowl, sprinkle with salt and let stand for 30 min. Drain and dry. Heat half the oil in a thick frying pan and brown the aubergine and courgette pieces, stirring lightly to brown on all sides, for 2–3 min. Using a slotted spoon, remove from pan or push to one side while you cook the sliced onions and peppers (be careful to remove all seeds) for about 10 min, adding remainder of oil. Add garlic and seasoning and combine onion mixture with aubergines and courgettes. Place slices of peeled tomatoes on top, sprinkle with chopped parsley, cover pan and cook for about 35 min, shaking pan occasionally, until all the excess juices have evaporated; be careful it does not catch on the bottom of the pan.

This can be cooked beforehand and re-heated just before serving if more convenient.

MUSHROOMS

Mushrooms are a most useful vegetable to use for hors-d'oeuvre and appetisers, and also for savouries to finish a meal instead of a sweet. They can be served both hot and cold, and are delicious either raw or cooked so I make no apologies for giving so many recipes using these excellent fungi which are obtainable at reasonable prices all through the year.

Mushrooms à la Grecque (serves 4–6)

There are a number of recipes for this very popular dish, which can be served as part of a selection of hors-d'oeuvre or as the first course for a family meal or a dinner party. It needs to be prepared at least 12 hr before serving.

	USA	Imperial	Metric
button mushrooms	2lb	2lb	800g
lemon juice	¼ lemon	¼ lemon	¼ lemon
wine vinegar	1¼ cups	½ pint	284ml
olive oil	8 tbsp	¼ pint	142ml
garlic, crushed	2 cloves	2 cloves	2 cloves
fresh thyme	2 sprigs	2 sprigs	2 sprigs
parsley	2 sprigs	2 sprigs	2 sprigs
bay leaf	1	1	1
whole peppercorns	6	6	6
parsley, finely chopped	2 tbsp	2 tbsp	2 tbsp

Trim stems and wash mushrooms in warm water, but do not peel. Drain well and put into a saucepan with lemon juice and just enough cold water to cover. Bring slowly to the boil, lower heat and simmer for 10 min. Drain well, and place in a shallow earthenware dish. Combine remainder of ingredients (except chopped parsley) in an enamel saucepan and bring to boil, then simmer gently for 20 min. Strain and pour this over mushrooms, cool and place in refrigerator for at least 12 hr before serving. Drain and sprinkle with finely chopped parsley.

The above recipe is one I collected in Athens after enjoying a big plate of mushrooms prepared in that way. The following recipe is another version of Mushrooms à la Grecque as it is made in the lovely island of Rhodes, which I also enjoyed, but which you will see is quite different.

Mushrooms à la Rhodes (serves 4–6)

	USA	Imperial	Metric
button mushrooms	1 lb	1 lb	400g
medium onions	2	2	2
tomatoes	1 lb	1 lb	400g
garlic, crushed	2 cloves	2 cloves	2 cloves
stock	1¼ cups	½ pint	284ml
olive oil	2 tbsp	2 tbsp	28ml
salt and pepper, to taste			
parsley, chopped	2 tbsp	2 tbsp	2 tbsp

Wash mushrooms in warm water, trim stalks but do not peel. Finely chop onions, peel tomatoes and chop. Heat oil in pan and lightly brown garlic on all sides, then discard. Brown onions lightly, add tomatoes and stock (may be made with bouillon cubes) and simmer for 20 min. Add mushrooms, season to taste and continue to cook gently for about 15 min, or until mushrooms are cooked and the mixture is not too moist.

Cool and serve sprinkled with finely chopped parsley.

If you have a home freezer this is an excellent recipe for freezing. Pack in plastic containers to freeze, and remember to defrost in refrigerator about 10 hr before serving.

Cheese-Stuffed Mushrooms (serves 8)

These are delicious as a rather different hors-d'oeuvre, and being low on calories are good for those watching the weight, whether it be pounds or kilos.

	USA	Imperial	Metric
mushrooms	24	24	24
cottage cheese	½ lb	½ lb	200g

26

onion, grated	1 tsp	1 tsp	1 tsp
curry powder	½ tsp	½ tsp	½ tsp
salt, pepper and paprika, to taste			

Choose large mushroom caps, as near the same size as possible. Remove stems (use to flavour a casserole) but do not peel. Pour boiling water over mushrooms to clean them, then drain well and dry. Blend together cheese, curry powder, onion, salt and pepper to taste and fill mushroom caps. Dust with paprika. Serve on crisp lettuce leaves, or on thick slices of peeled tomatoes, allowing 3 mushrooms for each serving.

If you prefer to serve these hot, use grated cheddar cheese instead of the cottage cheese and moisten with a little mayonnaise or cream, adding onion and curry powder as above. Put under a hot grill for a few minutes until bubbling. These need to be watched as they cook.

Mushroom Fritters (serves 4)

These are delicious, but as they must be served immediately after frying, don't include them on your menu unless you have somebody in the kitchen to cook them just before you sit down.

	USA	Imperial	Metric
button mushrooms	½lb	½lb	200g
flour	4 tbsp	2oz	50g
salt	1 tsp	1 tsp	1 tsp
oil	2 tsp	2 tsp	2 tsp
water	4 tbsp	2 fl oz	56ml
made mustard	2 tsp	2 tsp	2 tsp
Worcestershire sauce	2 tsp	2 tsp	2 tsp
egg white	1	1	1
oil, for frying			

The really small button mushrooms are best for these. Wipe over the tops with a damp cloth and trim the stems, but do not remove.

Sift flour and salt into a bowl, and make a well in the centre. Add mustard and liquids and gradually stir in the flour from the edges,

MUSHROOMS IN SOUR CREAM

beating until smooth. Beat egg white until stiff and fold into mixture. Have a small pan of deep oil heated to the point where a cube of bread turns golden in a minute. Dip mushrooms into batter a few at a time and fry in hot oil until golden brown. Drain on kitchen paper and serve at once with tartare sauce (*p* 120).

Mushrooms in Sour Cream (serves 6)

These can be prepared in the morning ready to be served for dinner at night. This is a recipe given to me by a Hungarian friend, and I have also enjoyed it in Yugoslavia.

	USA	Imperial	Metric
mushrooms	⅔lb	⅔lb	300g
dairy soured cream	1¼ cups	½ pint	284ml
canned pimentos, to garnish			

Choose fairly large button mushrooms and remove stems. Wash in boiling water, then drain well and dry. Slice fairly thin and mix with the soured cream, and stand in a cool place (not the refrigerator) until ready to serve.

Put into a shallow serving dish and garnish with strips of well-drained pimento, or divide between 6 individual serving dishes.

Mushrooms with Anchovies

Another version of the above dish uses well-drained anchovy fillets cut into thin strips and used as a garnish instead of the pimento. Sprinkle with finely chopped chives or parsley.

Italian Stuffed Mushrooms (serves 12)

I enjoyed these mushrooms as a first course of a splendid dinner at a farmhouse restaurant in the hills behind Alassio, and begged for the recipe. They can be prepared some time before cooking, but should be served straight from the oven.

	USA	Imperial	Metric
large mushrooms	24	24	24
butter	2 tbsp	1oz	25g
oil	2 tbsp	2 tbsp	28ml
onion, chopped	2 tbsp	2 tbsp	2 tbsp
dry sherry	2 tbsp	2 tbsp	28ml
tomatoes	3 medium	3 medium	3 medium
garlic	1 clove	1 clove	1 clove
soft breadcrumbs	¼ cup	1oz	25g
parsley, chopped	1 tbsp	1 tbsp	1 tbsp
salt and pepper, to taste			

Remove stems, wash and chop small. Wash mushroom caps in boiling water, drain and dry. Heat butter and half the oil in a frying pan, cook onion, finely chopped garlic and mushroom stems for 1 min. Add finely chopped tomatoes and cook for 3 min, then add breadcrumbs, parsley, salt and pepper and mix well. Stuff mushroom caps with this mixture, arrange in a greased baking dish large enough to take them all in one layer, and sprinkle with remainder of oil. Bake in a hot oven (425° F, 220° C, Gas Mark 7) for 10 min. Serve hot on rounds of fried bread. If cooking too quickly cover with a layer of foil.

Another version of the above recipe adds chopped ham to the mixture, and instead of crumbs cooked rice can be used.

Escargots Bourguignons (serves 4)

If you want to give your guests something really different for a change, try them with these—which are really snails in garlic butter. But be sure your friends are the adventurous type who will enjoy the idea of eating snails spiced with plenty of garlic. And they should only be served before a strongly flavoured main course.

You won't have to go out and catch your snails, as they come already prepared in tins, with a twin pack of nicely cleaned snail shells, but you do have to prepare the garlic butter, which can be done beforehand.

	USA	Imperial	Metric
canned snails with shells	24	24	24
butter	¾lb	¾lb	200g
garlic	3 cloves	3 cloves	3 cloves
parsley, chopped	3 tbsp	3 tbsp	3 tbsp
lemon juice	2 tsp	2 tsp	2 tsp
Worcestershire sauce	1 tsp	1 tsp	1 tsp
pepper, to taste			

Peel and crush garlic and blend with butter and all other ingredients, except the snails. Leave to stand in a cool place for at least 1 hr.

Open can of snails and the packet of shells, insert a little prepared butter into each shell, push the snail into the shell and cover with some more of the garlic butter, pressing into the shell. Stand the filled shells in small ovenproof dishes or ramekins, allowing 6 to a serving, then put into a hot oven (450° F, 230° C, Gas Mark 7) for 10–12 min, or until sizzling.

Serve with crusty bread to mop up the garlic butter in the dishes.

Persian Aubergine Soufflé (serves 6)

This is a rather exotic dish which can be served either hot or cold when the main dish is not too rich. For those who may not be familiar with the aubergine, sometimes called egg plant, it is a shiny, purple-skinned vegetable, usually egg-shaped, but sometimes to be found resembling a thick sausage. Much of the flavour is found in the skin, so it should not be peeled, but before cooking the excess moisture should be removed by cutting into desired pieces, sprinkling with salt and leaving, covered with a plate, for about 20 min. I usually place them in a colander for the moisture to drain away, then wash and dry well before cooking.

	USA	Imperial	Metric
aubergines	1¼lb	1¼lb	600g
salt and pepper, to taste			
cooking oil	3 tbsp	3 tbsp	42ml
lemon juice	2 tbsp	2 tbsp	28ml
garlic, crushed	1 clove	1 clove	1 clove

PERSIAN AUBERGINE SOUFFLÉ

	USA	Imperial	Metric
eggs	4	4	4
butter	1 tbsp	½oz	12½g
plain yoghurt	½ cup	4 fl oz	113ml
almonds, chopped	1 tbsp	1 tbsp	1 tbsp

Cut aubergine into about 6 slices, sprinkle with salt and leave for 20 min to drain, then wash and dry slices. Heat oil in pan and fry slices very gently (they burn easily) until golden and soft. Cool, then put into a blender with salt and pepper, lemon juice and garlic until smooth; or press through a sieve. Separate yolks and whites of the eggs, beat yolks very slightly and stir into aubergine. Whip whites until stiff and fold into the mixture.

Melt the butter in soufflé dish or deep oval casserole, pour in the mixture and put into a moderate oven (350° F, 180° C or Gas Mark 4) and bake for 30–40 min until firm to the touch. Put chopped nuts (walnuts can also be used if preferred) on to a piece of foil and toast in oven for last 10 min of baking time.

Remove dish from the oven and pour the yoghurt over the top, then sprinkle with the nuts and serve at once. Or if serving cold, leave soufflé to cool before adding yoghurt and nuts.

EGGS

Eggs can be used in a great variety of ways as starters for an interesting meal, or as part of a buffet lunch or dinner.

I can remember the late André Simon, who was as knowledgeable about food as he was about wine, telling me that few people knew how to cook hard boiled eggs, which was why so many of those used in restaurant dishes had tough, leathery whites and were hard to digest. 'They leave them on the stove cooking merrily away for half an hour, whereas ten minutes' simmering is quite enough—then they must be cooled quickly in cold water,' he told me.

I always add a little salt to the water just in case one of the eggs should break, and turn them over several times to keep the yolks centred.

31

Stuffed Savoury Eggs

These are always popular, whether served as part of an hors-d'oeuvre tray, as a first course on lettuce leaves and garnished with tomato or cucumber slices, or as part of a buffet table.

A great variety of fillings can be used, depending on what is available and the tastes of your guests, and here are just a few suggestions. I find when serving these as a first course that 3 half eggs are sufficient, but that is also a matter of taste.

Cook 12 eggs as directed above, shell and cut in halves crosswise. Cut a little slice from the end of each egg so that halves stand upright when filled. Carefully scoop out yolks into a basin and mash with selected fillings, or mix in electric blender until smooth. The egg whites can be filled from an icing bag or with a teaspoon, piling filling up over the top of the whites. Garnish each filled egg with a caper, a sprinkle of paprika or a square of canned pimento.

Anchovy Eggs: Put yolks of 12 eggs, 6 anchovy fillets, 1 tbsp chopped onion or chives, 3 tbsp mayonnaise (*p* 119), 1 tsp lemon juice into electric blender and blend until smooth. If not using a blender, mash yolks with mayonnaise, chop anchovies very fine and mix all other ingredients together until smooth. Season to taste and fill egg whites. Stand each filled egg on a slice of tomato. Serve extra mayonnaise separately.

Curried Eggs: Blend yolks of 12 eggs with 2 tsp curry powder, 1 tbsp chutney, 1 tsp lemon juice, 2–3 tbsp mayonnaise or cottage cheese, salt and pepper to taste. Fill egg halves and serve each one on a slice of either fresh or pickled cucumber. Garnish with pieces of pimento. Mayonnaise flavoured with a little curry powder can be served separately.

Hungarian Eggs: Blend or mash egg yolks with horseradish cream to taste, adding a little top of the milk if mixture is not creamy enough. Add finely chopped Hungarian salami with salt and pepper to taste. Fill egg halves and sprinkle each with paprika. Serve on crisp lettuce and garnish with slices of tomato.

Piquant Eggs: Chop mustard pickles as fine as possible and blend into yolks mashed with a little melted butter. Season to taste with salt and pepper. Fill egg halves and garnish each one with a caper.

Cheese and Tomato Eggs: Blend 12 egg yolks with ½ cup cottage cheese (4oz, 100g) and add enough tomato chutney or tomato ketchup to make a smooth paste. Season to taste with salt and pepper and a dash of cayenne. Serve on lettuce leaves with slices of tomato.

Belgian Eggs

These are so called because red, yellow and black are the official colours of Belgium. They are easy to prepare and inexpensive, and make an attractive beginning to a meal.

Scramble required number of eggs in the usual way and leave to get cold. Serve piled on top of slices of ripe, peeled tomatoes and garnish with thin slices of canned, drained anchovies.

Another version of this adds the chopped anchovies to the scrambled eggs, then when cold serves the eggs on top of tomato slices. Garnish each with a caper.

If preferred, the eggs can be served hot, on slices of grilled tomato, but in this case you need somebody preparing them in the kitchen, as they must be served immediately after cooking.

Oeufs Pochés en Tomates

This is a popular French hors-d'oeuvre which we would call Poached Eggs in Tomatoes, and although it seems very simple it can be a refreshing start for dinner, or a good addition to a buffet table.

Allow one egg for each serving, and they are best poached in metal rings or an individual poacher pan to give them a good shape. Allow to cool, and trim edges if necessary. Place each egg on a thick slice of tomato, season to taste and cover with mayonnaise (*p* 119) to which either chopped chives, capers, olives or pimento have been added. Chill well before serving.

Eggs Washington

Allow 1 tomato and 1 egg for each serving.

Cut a slice from the top of required number of tomatoes (choose all the same size), and carefully hollow out seeds and core. Season with salt and pepper and turn upside-down to drain. Chop up half an anchovy fillet for each tomato and place in each hollow, then break an

C   33

egg into each tomato. Put each tomato into small ovenproof ramekins or bun tins and bake in moderate oven (350° F, 180° C, Gas Mark 4) until egg is just set. Serve at once.

Copenhagen Eggs (serves 6)

Danish cooks prepare the most marvellous smørrebrød or cold tables, with the food arranged and garnished most beautifully. This is one way they serve eggs for their cold buffet, but these also make good hors-d'oeuvre.

	USA	Imperial	Metric
hard boiled eggs	6	6	6
dairy soured cream	¼ cup	4 fl oz	113ml
mayonnaise (p 119)	4 tbsp	2 fl oz	56ml
curry powder	1 tsp	1 tsp	1 tsp
shrimps, shelled	¼lb	¼lb	100g
chives, chopped	1 tbsp	1 tbsp	1 tbsp
lettuce leaves			
paprika, to garnish			

Blend together mayonnaise, curry powder, chives, sour cream and chopped shrimps and stand in a cool place for at least 30 min. When ready to serve shell eggs and cut in halves, and arrange 2 halves, cut side down, on crisp lettuce leaves on 6 small plates. Cover with shrimp mayonnaise, sprinkle with a little paprika and serve at once.

Stuffed Tomatoes (serves 6)

Tomatoes look most attractive as a first course when filled with a tasty mixture. Choose evenly sized tomatoes, ripe but quite firm. Cut a slice from the top of each one, scoop out the pulp and sprinkle insides with salt and pepper, and turn upside-down to drain for half an hour before filling with any of the mixtures here. Allow one to a serving, place on a crisp lettuce cup on individual plates.

Cheese and Olives: Blend together ½lb (200g) cottage cheese with 1 tsp grated onion and 2 tbsp chopped black or green olives. Season to taste with salt and pepper. Pile into prepared tomato cases and serve as above.

Cheese and Celery: As above recipe but instead of olives add chop
celery and chopped red pepper.
Cheese and Pickled Cucumbers: As in first recipe but in place of olives
add 2 large dill pickled cucumbers, chopped. Sprinkle with paprika.
All these should be chilled after filling.

Tomatoes Fines Herbes (serves 8)

This is a delicious 'starter' for those who have fresh herbs growing in
their gardens, and is just right for a summer evening's buffet meal.

	USA	Imperial	Metric
large ripe tomatoes	8	8	8
parsley, finely chopped	8 tbsp	8 tbsp	8 tbsp
onion or chives, finely chopped	4 tbsp	4 tbsp	4 tbsp
basil, finely chopped	2 tbsp	2 tbsp	2 tbsp
tarragon, finely chopped	2 tbsp	2 tbsp	2 tbsp
garlic, finely chopped	1 clove	1 clove	1 clove
wine vinegar	2–3 tbsp	2–3 tbsp	2–3 tbsp
olive oil	6–7 tbsp	6–7 tbsp	6–7 tbsp
salt, pepper and sugar, to taste			
mayonnaise (p 119)	1 cup	8 fl oz	226ml
lettuce cups			

Choose round, well-shaped tomatoes, as nearly the same size as
possible. Place in boiling water for a minute or two, drain and peel,
then cut each in 4 thick slices, keeping the slices together.

Mix together all the chopped herbs, seasonings and vinegar, stirring
enough oil in to make a thick green paste. Put aside a quarter of this
mixture, and use remainder to sandwich together the tomato slices,
re-forming them as whole tomatoes. Chill until ready to serve. Place
each tomato in a lettuce cup on individual plates.

Mix remaining herb mixture with the mayonnaise some time before
serving to allow flavours to blend, and serve separately.

Another version of these tomatoes adds chopped capers to the herb
mixture.

Salads for Starters

A colourful, well-arranged salad makes a very acceptable starter for a good meal, but care should be taken in choosing the ingredients so they do not clash with the main course. You would not serve a chicken salad for a starter if the main course was poultry, or a salad such as the Salade Niçoise (*p* 39) if fish was being served as the main dish, or pineapple had been planned for the sweet.

A simple salad can be made into something really special by a good dressing, and a choice of these can be found on pages 119-22.

Always have salad ingredients such as lettuce as fresh and crisp as possible. Cook extra peas or beans for dinner the day before and serve the left-overs as part of a salad.

For a dinner party individual salads look attractive, and can usually be arranged better, but do not smother them with dressing or mayonnaise in case some people do not like dressings. Instead serve these separately for guests to help themselves.

Strawberry and Cheese Salad

An unusual combination as the first course for a dinner party when

36

strawberries are in season, or serve them on picks as part of a buffet party spread.

Choose large, ripe berries and cut each one in halves lengthwise. Blend cream cheese with a little top of milk until smooth and light and use to sandwich the halved strawberries together. Chill until ready to serve, then place two or three berries on a slice of peeled orange for each serving and arrange on a crisp lettuce leaf.

Salada Valenciana

This colourful salad is easy to make, and comes from a splendid restaurant in Valencia, Spain, called Cesareo's, where they serve a delicious collection of entremeses, from which this recipe comes, and also the best paella I have tasted in all Spain.

For each serving arrange 4 slices peeled ripe tomatoes alternately with 4 slices peeled orange on small plates. Beat cottage cheese with enough orange juice to make a good consistency, season with salt and pepper to taste. Spoon over above, then sprinkle with finely chopped black olives.

Minted Cucumber Salad (serves 4)

Wonderful for those on a slimming diet.

	USA	Imperial	Metric
young cucumber	1	1	1
plain yoghurt	1 cup	8oz	200g
onion, finely chopped	1 tbsp	1 tbsp	1 tbsp
mint, finely chopped	1 tbsp	1 tbsp	1 tbsp
salt and pepper, to taste			
lemon juice	1 tsp	1 tsp	1 tsp

Peel cucumber and cut into dice, put into a strainer and sprinkle with salt. Leave to drain for 30 min, then wipe dry. Mix with all other ingredients and chill well before serving.

This looks attractive served in goblets, each one garnished with a sprig of mint, or it can be added to an hors-d'oeuvre tray.

Butter Bean Salad (serves 4–5)

This can be served as a first course by itself, or included in a mixed hors-d'oeuvre platter.

	USA	Imperial	Metric
dried butter beans	½lb	½lb	200g
small onion	1	1	1
bay leaf	1	1	1
salt and pepper, to taste			
creamed horseradish	1 tbsp	1 tbsp	1 tbsp
yoghurt	½ cup	4 fl oz	113ml
canned pimento, chopped	1 tbsp	1 tbsp	1 tbsp

Wash the beans well, cover with cold water and leave overnight to soak. Next day add peeled onion, bay leaf and a little salt and if necessary some more water to ensure that beans are covered by about 2in (5cm). Bring to the boil, then reduce heat and simmer for about an hour or until tender but not so soft that they break up. Drain well, remove onion and bay leaf and leave to cool. When cool, stir horseradish into yoghurt and add beans, season with salt and pepper to taste. Chop pimento and sprinkle over the top.

Quick Butter Bean Salad (serves 4–5)

When you haven't the time to prepare beans overnight, a simple salad can be made with canned butter beans or broad beans.

	USA	Imperial	Metric
canned butter beans	15oz	15oz	425g
chives or parsley, chopped	2 tbsp	2 tbsp	2 tbsp
pimento, chopped	2 tbsp	2 tbsp	2 tbsp
sauce vinaigrette (p 122), to cover			

Drain beans well and combine with all other ingredients at least ½ hr before serving.

Grated raw carrot can be substituted for the pimento if preferred.

Salade Niçoise (serves 6)

This is a classic Mediterranean hors-d'oeuvre, known everywhere and with countless variations, but this is the one I like best. Make it in a large rather shallow salad bowl and let guests help themselves.

	USA	Imperial	Metric
green string beans	1lb	1lb	400g
olive oil	5 tbsp	5 tbsp	70ml
wine vinegar	2 tbsp	2 tbsp	28ml
tuna fish	7½oz can	7½oz can	212g
hard boiled eggs	3	3	3
black olives, to taste			
anchovy fillets	12	12	12
crisp lettuce	1 large	1 large	1 large
sauce vinaigrette (p 122)			

Chop beans into ½in (1cm) pieces and cook in boiling, salted water for 10 min. Drain well and cool, then mix with oil and vinegar some time before serving.

Line a salad bowl with crisp lettuce leaves. Drain tuna, remove any bones and black skin and flake into fairly large pieces, then mix lightly with beans. Put these in centre of bowl, surround with a ring of quartered eggs and black olives, then place the drained anchovy fillets on top radiating from the centre like the spokes of a wheel. Serve sauce vinaigrette separately.

This can be varied by adding capers or chopped parsley, strips of canned pimento or fresh green pepper, sliced or quartered tomatoes, just as you please.

Salade Menton

This is nearly the same as the above, but in place of the beans use diced cucumber which has been salted and left to drain for 30 min, then wiped dry. Replace the egg with quarters of peeled tomatoes.

Sunomono (serves 6)

This recipe comes from the wife of the Governor of Pago Pago,

American Samoa, and is a popular starter for one of her summer night dinners.

	USA	Imperial	Metric
cucumbers	2 medium	2 medium	2 medium
salt	1 tbsp	1 tbsp	1 tbsp
cider vinegar	4 tbsp	4 tbsp	56ml
water	1 tbsp	1 tbsp	1 tbsp
sugar	⅟ tsp	⅟ tsp	⅟ tsp
sake or sherry	1 tsp	1 tsp	1 tsp
shrimps or crab	3 tbsp	3 tbsp	3 tbsp

Peel cucumber thinly, slice into quarters lengthwise and remove seeds, then cut into fingers. Place in a bowl and sprinkle with the salt, then place a flat dish that will fit inside bowl on top of cucumbers to weight them down. Stand for 1–2 hr, then drain off liquid that has collected. Divide cucumbers into 6 small bowls and garnish with a few shrimps or flaked crabmeat. Mix together cider vinegar, water, sugar and sake or sherry and sprinkle over the top. Serve chilled.

AVOCADOS

Having lived in such places as Australia, South Africa and the Canary Islands where it is quite usual to have several avocado trees in your garden to provide you with a plentiful supply of these exotic fruit, I have found many ways to serve them both as a beginning and as an ending to a good dinner.

Having a bland flavour, the avocado can be combined with different ingredients to give a delicious first course, but care should be taken not to 'swamp' this individual taste by adding a much stronger flavour. Personally, I prefer to season it with a little pepper and lemon juice only, or a good vinaigrette dressing, but I do know people who cannot eat an avocado unless it comes with prawns, or smoked salmon, so it is all a matter of personal taste.

You can tell if an avocado is ripe by rolling it gently between the hands to see if it is soft. If buying a few days before it is to be eaten,

choose a firm—but not hard—avocado and leave in the kitchen t_
ripen, but do not put in the refrigerator. A wrapped avocado will
ripen quicker. Always brush the cut surface with lemon juice to
prevent discolouring.

Andalucian Avocado

This is the way they serve avocados in Jerez, the sherry capital of Spain.
Prepare them about ½ hr before serving, and chill lightly. These amounts
are for 1 avocado, which is 2 servings.

	USA	Imperial	Metric
avocado	1	1	1
dry sherry	2 tbsp	2 tbsp	28ml
lemon juice	2 tsp	2 tsp	2 tsp
Worcestershire sauce	¼ tsp	¼ tsp	¼ tsp
salt and pepper, to taste			

Combine sherry, lemon juice, sauce, salt and pepper and shake well
together in a jar. These amounts can be multiplied according to the
number of avocados served.

Cut avocado in halves and remove seed. Slash the cut surface in a
crisscross pattern and pour in half the dressing, swirling it round to
coat the cut surface of each half to prevent discolouring.

If fresh lime juice is available, use in place of lemon juice.

Avocado and Grapefruit Martinique

Allow ½ avocado and ¼ grapefruit for each serving, with rum and
sugar to taste.

The night before serving, cut grapefruit in halves and cut out the
pulp, removing all white pith and membranes, and chop pulp into
pieces. Put into a bowl with some rum and sugar to taste and leave in
refrigerator. Chill avocados, and when ready to serve cut in halves and
remove seeds. Brush over cut surfaces with some of the grapefruit
juices to prevent discolouring, then fill hollows in each avocado with
chopped grapefruit. Garnish each with a cocktail cherry.

For those who like a dressing with their avocados, add the juices from the grapefruit to thick mayonnaise (*p* 119) blending together until smooth.

Surfer's Paradise Avocados (serves 6)

This recipe comes from one of the luxury hotels of the Queensland coast of Australia, and is a delicious combination to serve as a first course for a dinner party.

	USA	Imperial	Metric
avocados	2	2	2
naval oranges	2	2	2
shrimps, shelled	¼lb	4oz	100g
mayonnaise (p 119)	¾ cup	6oz	170ml
tomato purée or paste	1 tbsp	1 tbsp	1 tbsp
Worcestershire sauce	½ tsp	½ tsp	½ tsp
Tabasco sauce, few drops			
lettuce, shredded	6 tbsp	6 tbsp	6 tbsp

Peel oranges, removing all traces of white pith, and cut into slices. Halve avocados, remove stones, and peel as thinly as possible. Cut into slices crosswise. Mix together mayonnaise, both sauces and tomato purée or paste, beating together until smooth and blended. Add shelled shrimps.

Put a layer of shredded lettuce in the bottom of 6 glasses or sweet dishes. Round the inside edge of each glass arrange alternate slices of avocado and orange, then fill the middle with the shrimp mayonnaise.

Dressed Artichoke Hearts (serves 4–5)

Canned artichoke hearts make an unusual hors-d'oeuvre which can be prepared in a hurry, and served on individual plates, or they can be added to a mixed plate of hors-d'oeuvre.

	USA	Imperial	Metric
canned artichoke hearts	2 7oz cans	2 7oz cans	2 198g cans
French dressing (p 122)	4 tbsp	4 tbsp	56ml
tomatoes	4	4	4
parsley, chopped	2 tbsp	2 tbsp	2 tbsp

Peel and slice the tomatoes and arrange in a circle round 4 individual serving plates. Drain the artichoke hearts and divide between the 4 plates, placing in the middle of the tomatoes. Coat with French dressing and sprinkle with finely chopped parsley.

If preferred, use mayonnaise (*p* 119) in place of the French dressing. Serve with thinly sliced brown bread and butter.

Avocado Mousse (serves 6)

This can be made the day before, or at least 6 hr before serving, to give it time to chill and set properly. It looks attractive set in a fancy mould, or you can use a ring mould and fill the centre with the shrimps. Always turn out gelatine-set moulds on to a chilled plate for serving.

	USA	Imperial	Metric
ripe avocados	2 large	2 large	2 large
hot chicken stock	5 fl oz	$\frac{1}{4}$ pint	142ml
gelatine	$\frac{1}{2}$oz	$\frac{1}{2}$oz	12$\frac{1}{2}$g
lemon juice	1 tbsp	1 tbsp	1 tbsp
garlic, chopped	1 clove	1 clove	1 clove
double cream	5 fl oz	$\frac{1}{4}$ pint	142ml
mayonnaise (p 119)	5 fl oz	$\frac{1}{4}$ pint	142ml
prawns or shrimps, shelled	4oz	4oz	100g
salt and pepper, to taste			
ripe, peeled tomatoes, as required			

If you have an electric blender use it to make this. Put hot chicken stock (this can be made with a cube) and gelatine into container and blend until dissolved. Cut avocados in halves and remove stones, then cut out the pulp, scraping out the dark green part near the skin as this gives a good colour. Chop this pulp and add to container with lemon juice, garlic and mayonnaise and blend all together until smooth and free from lumps. Add this to the lightly whipped cream and blend all together. Season to taste. Pour into a lightly oiled mould or basin, cover with foil and chill until set firmly. Turn out on to a chilled erving plate and garnish with slices of peeled tomatoes topped with shrimps or prawns.

Extra mayonnaise can be handed round separately.

Summer Tomato Aspic (serves 4–5)

This makes a good beginning for a summer meal, something cool and attractive-looking, and has the added advantage that it can be made up well before serving time. The aspic can be set in an oblong mould and cut in slices at the table, or it can be divided between 4 or 5 small fancy moulds and turned out on crisp lettuce leaves for individual servings. For special occasions garnish with shrimps.

	USA	Imperial	Metric
tomato juice	16oz can	16oz can	454ml can
gelatine	1 tbsp	1 tbsp	1 tbsp
white wine vinegar	2 tsp	2 tsp	2 tsp
lemon juice	1 tbsp	1 tbsp	1 tbsp
whole peppercorns	4–5	4–5	4–5
bay leaf	$\frac{1}{2}$	$\frac{1}{2}$	$\frac{1}{2}$
onion, chopped	1 tbsp	1 tbsp	1 tbsp
fresh thyme, parsley and tarragon, few sprigs			
sugar, if liked	1 tsp	1 tsp	1 tsp
mayonnaise (p 119), as required			

Heat tomato juice with onion, bay leaf, herbs and peppercorns, simmering gently for 5 min, covered, then strain. Soak gelatine in a little water, then stir into hot tomato juice, Add vinegar, lemon juice and sugar if using, stir well, and pour into oblong mould or individual moulds.

When set, turn out on lettuce leaves and garnish with alternate slices of peeled tomatoes and cucumber. Serve mayonnaise (p 119) separately.

An alternative recipe for this is to pour a thin layer of tomato aspic in the bottom of an oblong mould and chill it until set firmly. On top of this layer arrange 4oz (100g) peeled shrimps and pour in remainder of aspic which has been kept liquid over hot water. Chill until set firmly, turn out on lettuce leaves or on a bed of sliced cucumber and cut in slices to serve. Serve mayonnaise separately.

Pâtés &
Savoury Dips

A slice of well-flavoured pâté makes a splendid beginning to a meal, and you can either make your own at least a day before it is to be served, or use any of the good-quality canned pâtés available. You can also buy a good variety of packaged pâtés prepared in sausage shapes. Both these latter types benefit from a little 'partying up' as in the directions that follow, and they look much nicer if served in small individual pottery bowls.

Serve pâté with thin slices of hot, freshly made toast (be sure and remove the crusts) and it is a good idea to use a napkin-lined basket to keep the toast hot when serving.

You can bring the pâté to the table in the terrine or container it has been cooked in, or turn it out and cut in slices, serving a slice on a plate lined with well-dried lettuce and garnished with pickled gherkins cut into fans or sliced dill pickles.

Home-made pâté will keep for a week in the refrigerator, and it can be frozen, but loses some of its original texture.

An electric blender makes the job of preparing pâté mixtures much easier, but several good cooks I know swear by an old-fashioned mortar and pestle for making their pâtés. Or you may use a household mincer with the fine blade, and put the mixture through twice to get the desired consistency.

Quick Liver Pâté

Either canned or packaged liver pâté can be given a luxury touch if prepared like this. Use an electric blender if available, or chop very finely, and pack mixture into small individual bowls.

Put the pâté into blender with 2 or 3 hard boiled eggs, 1 tbsp cream and 1 or 2 tbsp brandy or dry sherry and blend until smooth. Season to taste and serve garnished with chopped parsley.

Another variation of the above recipe is to omit the cream and add 4oz (100g) cream cheese to mixture in the blender.

Chicken Liver Pâté (serves 4)

This is a simple recipe using chicken livers as the main ingredient. Make it the day before serving and keep in refrigerator until ready to use.

	USA	Imperial	Metric
chicken livers	½lb	½lb	200g
butter	½ cup	4oz	100g
brandy or dry sherry	1 tbsp	1 tbsp	1 tbsp
onion, chopped	2 tbsp	2 tbsp	2 tbsp
salt, pepper and grated nutmeg, to taste			

Trim the chicken livers. Melt half the butter in a pan and cook chicken livers and onion gently for about 5 min, covered, shaking them occasionally. Put chicken livers, onion and the juices from the pan through the fine blade of the mincer, or an electric blender, adding brandy or sherry. Cream remaining butter and add liver mixture, beating thoroughly until well mixed, and seasoning to taste. If using a blender, the butter can be melted and added to the mixture in the blender with the brandy or sherry.

Divide mixture into 4 small dishes or a suitable serving dish and chill until ready to serve.

Liver Pâté (serves 6)
Make this the day before it is to be served.

	USA	Imperial	Metric
lamb's liver	½lb	½lb	200g
onion, chopped	2 tbsp	2 tbsp	2 tbsp
garlic	1 clove	1 clove	1 clove
pork sausage meat	½lb	½lb	200g
egg	1	1	1
parsley, chopped	1 tbsp	1 tbsp	1 tbsp
dried mixed herbs	½ tsp	½ tsp	½ tsp
streaky bacon	4 slices	4 rashers	4 slices
salt and pepper, to taste			

Soak the liver in cold water for 10 min, drain well and remove tubes. Put through the mincer, using the fine blade, with the onion and peeled garlic, then put through again with the sausage meat. With a fork, mix in lightly beaten egg, seasonings, parsley and herbs until thoroughly blended.

Use a 2½ cup (1 pint, 568ml) ovenproof casserole or terrine with a lid; butter the inside well and line base with the trimmed bacon slices. Fill dish with the pâté mixture, levelling off the top, and cover with remaining bacon slices. Cover with a piece of buttered paper or foil and then the lid. Stand dish in a baking tin containing about 1in (2½cm) cold water and bake in a moderately hot oven (375° F, 190° C, Gas Mark 5) for 1½ hr. Remove from oven and take off lid, then place a plate on top of the paper or foil with a weight on top to press it down. Cool and then put into refrigerator until ready to serve.

The pâté can be served from the terrine or casserole, or turned out on to a plate and cut in slices.

If preferred, pork liver can be used, or half pork and half lamb. A little brandy or sherry can be added for extra flavour.

Page 49 (*above*) Avocado with seafood cocktail (*below*) tomatoes with cheese and olive filling

Mixed Liver Pâté (serves 4–5)

This is a mixture of 3 kinds of liver, and is easily made in an electric blender, or it can be put through the fine blade of the mincer.

	USA	Imperial	Metric
chicken livers	¼lb	¼lb	100g
pig's liver	¼lb	¼lb	100g
calf or lamb's liver	1lb	1lb	400g
butter or bacon fat	¼ cup	2oz	50g
egg	1	1	1
garlic	1 clove	1 clove	1 clove
lemon juice	1 tbsp	1 tbsp	1 tbsp
brandy or stock	2 tbsp	2 tbsp	2 tbsp
salt and pepper, to taste			
streaky bacon	6 slices	6 rashers	6 slices
bay leaf	1	1	1

Soak the liver for 10 min in cold water, drain and trim, and chop coarsely. Fry in the butter or bacon fat until lightly browned, turning to cook evenly. Put liver and juices in the pan into the blender with the egg, garlic, lemon juice, brandy and seasoning, and blend for about 30 sec until smooth. If your blender has only a small container it may be necessary to do this in two lots, as the blender should never be more than ⅔ full.

Line an oval terrine or a loaf tin with half the bacon slices, pack the liver mixture into the terrine and place the bay leaf on top, then cover with remainder of bacon slices. Cover with foil or buttered paper, then with a lid, and place in a baking tin with a little water. Bake in a moderate oven (350° F, 180° C, Gas Mark 4) for about 1¼ hr.

When cooked, place a weighted plate on top of the foil and leave overnight.

Don't forget to remove the bay leaf before serving.

Patsy's Pâté (serves 4–5)

This is a recipe I first tasted at a house party in Cornwall, and as my

nostess had no name for it we called it after her. It is a very good way
of using up cold meat and is best made a day or so before serving for
flavours to blend. Either cooked beef, lamb or veal can be used as the
main ingredient.

	USA	Imperial	Metric
cooked meat	½lb	½lb	200g
pork sausage meat	½lb	½lb	200g
stale white bread	2 slices	2 slices	2 slices
milk	2 tbsp	2 tbsp	2 tbsp
onion, chopped	3 tbsp	3 tbsp	3 tbsp
parsley, chopped	2 tbsp	2 tbsp	2 tbsp
mixed herbs	½ tsp	½ tsp	½ tsp
egg yolks	2	2	2
salt, pepper and mustard, to taste			
gherkins or olives, to garnish			

Put cooked meat through the mincer, then put through again with
the onion, parsley and sausage meat. Cut crusts from bread slices and
soak them in the milk, then squeeze almost dry. Mix with the meat
mixture, adding herbs, egg yolks and seasonings and blending well
together. Pack into a well-buttered ovenproof dish, cover with foil or
buttered paper, then a lid, and stand dish in a baking tin containing a
little water. Bake in a moderate oven (350° F, 180° C, Gas Mark 4) for
1 hr. Cool and store in refrigerator until needed.

Turn out of dish and serve in slices with gherkins or olives and slices
of hot toast.

FISH PÂTÉS

In addition to pâtés made with meat there are some very good ones
with fish as the basic ingredient. These have the added advantage that
they can be made in an electric blender very easily and quickly and
need no cooking, or they can be rubbed through a sieve or pounded in
a mortar and pestle. Like the meat pâtés, they are improved by being
made the day before serving, and should be served with hot toast,
garnished with lemon quarters and sliced pickled cucumbers or gherkins.

Most canned fish such as salmon, tuna, sardines, mackerel or herrings, smoked fish such as cod, kipper or buckling, fresh or frozen shrimps or prawns can all be made into pâtés to serve as good beginnings to tasty meals.

Tuna Pâté in Lemon Cups (serves 4)

Made with canned tuna, this pâté is served in lemon cups for a dinner party. The same idea can be followed with any of the fish pâtés given here.

	USA	Imperial	Metric
canned tuna in oil	7oz	7oz	196g
butter	3 tbsp	1½oz	37½g
lemon juice	2 tsp	2 tsp	2 tsp
oil	2 tbsp	2 tbsp	2 tbsp
brandy or sherry	1 tbsp	1 tbsp	1 tbsp
parsley	4–5 sprigs	4–5 sprigs	4–5 sprigs
dried tarragon	pinch	pinch	pinch
(or fresh if available)			
freshly ground black pepper, to taste			

Drain oil from tuna and put 2 tbsp into the blender—discard remainder. Flake tuna roughly and put into blender with all other ingredients, blend until smooth. Turn into basin and chill.

Just before serving time scrub 4 large lemons, cut a thin slice from each end of each lemon so they will stand straight, and with a sharp-pointed teaspoon scoop out all the flesh and juice. (This can be used for another recipe for which lemon juice is required, simply pressing out the juice.) Fill lemon cups with the chilled pâté and serve.

Herring Pâté (serves 4)

	USA	Imperial	Metric
canned boneless herrings	7oz can	7oz can	196g can
butter	3 tbsp	1½oz	37½g
lemon juice	1 tbsp	1 tbsp	1 tbsp

	USA	Imperial	Metric
Worcestershire sauce	1 tbsp	1 tbsp	1 tbsp
salt and pepper, to taste			

Cream the butter and mash the drained fish, then combine the two, blending in remaining ingredients until smooth. Divide between 4 small dishes or containers and chill.

Garnish each with a ½ lemon slice tucked into one side, and serve with thin slices of brown bread and butter.

Canned sardines or sild (small herrings) can be substituted for the herrings, but remove their tails before mashing.

Norwegian Prawn Pâté (serves 6)

Norwegians have excellent prawns, and even though they export a great deal of these succulent shell fish, they also use them in many ways in their own cuisine. This pâté is one recipe I collected there. Either fresh or frozen shelled prawns can be used, but defrost the frozen ones before starting to make the pâté.

	USA	Imperial	Metric
prawns, shelled	½lb	½lb	200g
butter	½ cup	4oz	100g
lemon juice	1 tbsp	1 tbsp	1 tbsp
parsley, chopped	1 tbsp	1 tbsp	1 tbsp
salt and pepper, to taste			
tomato paste, to taste			

My hostess in Bergen pounded the prawns in a pestle and mortar until they were a smooth paste, but a blender will do the job much quicker if you have one, putting all ingredients except tomato paste into the blender until smooth. Taste for seasoning and add just enough tomato paste to give the pâté a good colour. Divide between 6 small dishes or bowls and chill well. This pâté looks most attractive if served in lemon cups as described on page 53.

SAVOURY DIPS

For buffet parties or informal dinners these savoury dips are both tasty and easy to serve—a kind of do-it-yourself hors-d'oeuvre.

These dips are very simple to make, and I am giving here a basic recipe for savoury dips which can be varied by adding different ingredients. These ingredients can be changed depending on the time of year and whether or not they are easily available in the shops.

Serve each dip in a bowl placed in the centre of a large platter, and then surround it with either fingers of freshly made toast or with small plain crackers. Potato crisps can also be used.

Alternatively, another method of serving is to circle the bowl with fingers of raw carrot, sticks of celery or fingers of cucumber. Guests can then use these pieces of vegetable to help themselves to the dip.

Several varieties of dips or spreads can be served at the same time, but be sure they are each quite different in flavour. For instance, you would not serve 2 dips made with cheese at the same time, just as a dip made with sardines and another using tuna would not be advisable at the same meal.

An electric blender is a great boon when preparing these dips and spreads. There are also a number of excellent packaged dips on the market which are very simple to make up when you are in a hurry.

If possible, all these dips should be made up several hours before they are to be served, then stored in the refrigerator to allow the flavours to mature.

Basic Dip

	USA	Imperial	Metric
cottage cheese	¼lb	¼lb	200g
double cream	½ cup	4 fl oz	113ml
salt and pepper, to taste			
Worcestershire sauce	2 tsp	2 tsp	2 tsp

Additions:

2oz (50g) finely chopped peeled shrimps and 2 tbsp (28ml) tomato ketchup.

3 tbsp chopped chutney, 1 tsp curry powder and 2 heaped tbsp chopped chives or spring onions.

2 tbsp (28ml) lemon juice, 1 tbsp grated onion, ½ tsp paprika and 3 tbsp stoned and chopped black or green olives.

As above, but substitute 6 finely chopped anchovy fillets for the chopped olives.

Beat cream until thick, then mix in the cottage cheese and seasonings, adding any of the above ingredients.

Cheese Dips (makes 2 cups)

To a basic mixture of ½lb (200g) cottage cheese and 5 fl oz (142ml) either mayonnaise (p 119) or soured cream, add any of the following flavourings:

2oz (50g) chopped, peeled shrimps and 2 tbsp tomato ketchup.

2 heaped tbsp chopped chives or spring onions.

2 heaped tbsp each chopped canned pimento and chopped celery.

3–4 chopped anchovies and a dash of cayenne pepper.

2 tsp curry powder and 3 tbsp chopped chutney, with 2 tsp lemon juice.

Blend cottage cheese and mayonnaise or soured cream together until smooth, then add flavouring.

Stuffed Edam Cheese Dip

If you don't know, Edam cheese is the round Dutch cheese with a bright red casing, usually weighing about 4lb. It looks most decorative, and makes an attractive addition to a buffet party table when hollowed out and stuffed as in the following recipe—for a party of 12 I usually allow at least 2 cheeses, one at each end of the table. Place the prepared cheese in the middle of a serving platter and surround with carrot and celery sticks and small crackers.

	USA	Imperial	Metric
Baby Edam cheese	4lb	4lb	1·8kg
butter	¼ cup	4oz	100g

	USA	Imperial	Metric
grated onion	*1 tbsp*	*1 tbsp*	*1 tbsp*
dry mustard	*½ tsp*	*½ tsp*	*½ tsp*
beer	*½ pint*	*8 fl oz*	*226ml*
stuffed olives, to garnish			

Cut a slice from the top of the cheese, and with a sharp-pointed teaspoon scoop out the cheese, leaving a firm shell. Put chopped cheese and butter in blender container with a little beer, and blend until smooth, then add remainder of beer with the onion and mustard and blend again until well mixed. Pile this mixture into the Edam shell, leave in a cool place for at least an hour before serving. Garnish top with sliced olives.

Cheese and Celery Dip (makes 2 cups)

	USA	Imperial	Metric
cream of celery soup	*15oz can*	*15oz can*	*375g can*
Danish Blue cheese	*¼lb*	*¼lb*	*100g*
Cheddar cheese, grated	*¼lb*	*¼lb*	*100g*
Worcestershire sauce	*2 tsp*	*2 tsp*	*2 tsp*
pepper, to taste			

Put all ingredients into blender until smooth. For a change use cream of tomato soup in place of the celery.

Viennese Dip (makes 2 cups)

	USA	Imperial	Metric
cottage cheese	*½lb*	*½lb*	*200g*
hard boiled egg yolks	*2*	*2*	*2*
mayonnaise (p 119)	*2 tbsp*	*2 tbsp*	*2 tbsp*
onion, grated	*1 tbsp*	*1 tbsp*	*1 tbsp*
French mustard	*1 tsp*	*1 tsp*	*1 tsp*
anchovy fillets	*4*	*4*	*4*
paprika, to taste			

Put into blender until smooth, or beat first 5 ingredients together and add chopped anchovies, and paprika to taste.
Instead of paprika, chopped canned pimento can be added.

Tuna Dip (makes 3 cups)

	USA	Imperial	Metric
tuna	2 7oz cans	2 7oz cans	350g
cottage cheese	½lb	½lb	200g
dry sherry	2 tbsp	2 tbsp	2 tbsp
onion, grated	1 tbsp	1 tbsp	1 tbsp
top milk	3 tbsp	3 tbsp	3 tbsp
Worcestershire sauce	1 tbsp	1 tbsp	1 tbsp
parsley, chopped	2 tbsp	2 tbsp	2 tbsp
black pepper, to taste			

Put all ingredients through blender until smooth, or beat all well together.

Guacamole (makes 2 cups)

This is a recipe from Mexico which makes an unusual party dip when avocados are available. There are several variations of this receipe, so choose the one you prefer.

	USA	Imperial	Metric
avocados	2	2	2
lemon juice	2 tbsp	2 tbsp	2 tbsp
ripe tomatoes	2 large	2 large	2 large
onion, grated	2 tbsp	2 tbsp	2 tbsp
chili powder	1 tsp	1 tsp	1 tsp
salt and pepper, to taste			

Cut avocados in halves, remove stones and peel as thinly as possible, then cube the pulp. Peel and chop tomatoes. Put all ingredients into blender until smooth. If no blender is available rub mixture through a sieve. Chill in a covered dish until ready to serve, accompanied by crisp crackers or crisps.

Vary the above mixture by adding either ½lb (200g) cream cheese or 2 finely chopped hard boiled eggs, and blending well. Chopped pickled cucumber or chopped canned pimento can be added just before serving.

Soups, Hot & Cold

A famous gastronome once likened the soup course to the overture of an opera, saying that it must be in harmony with the rest of the meal.

This rule still applies to our everyday meals as well as more important dinner parties. It is not good planning to serve a creamy soup and then follow it with a dish such as fish in white sauce, or a chicken fricassée, just as it would be bad to follow a rich brown soup with a highly flavoured meat course.

Most soups are fairly easy to make, especially those made with vegetables, and a pressure cooker is a great boon. On the other hand, do not despise canned and packaged soups which can be obtained today in so many flavours that they are a great help to the busy cook. And those who have gone through the somewhat tiresome procedure of making consommé will appreciate the convenience of the really good canned consommé available, which sets to a good thick jelly when left in the refrigerator, and looks and tastes very good when served iced on a summer's day.

Remember that soup is not just a winter dish, for it can make a very pleasant beginning to a summer meal; but just as hot soup must be *really hot* during the winter, so must cold soup be *really iced* in the summer.

The variety of soups which can be served for both everyday and special meals is very wide, and the cuisine of many countries has given us interesting and flavoursome recipes to add to our own favourites. If you have not already tried them experiment with such good soups as Russian Borsch, which can be served either hot or cold; Italian Suppa di Castagne made with chestnuts; French Onion Soup; Japanese Chicken and Mushroom, or Spanish Gazpacho, all of which you will find in the following pages.

Soup bowls or cups are preferable for serving either hot or cold soup rather than the old-fashioned soup plates, as the smaller area keeps the soup hot longer. Stand the soup bowl or cup on a plate before serving —not just on the table. I like the idea of place plates as used by many hostesses for dinner parties, a large plate which need not match your dinner plates, and which is left in place all through dinner. One clever hostess I know has collected her place plates from all over the world; none match but they are nearly all the same size, and they make a wonderful conversation starter if guests do not all know each other.

A soup tureen is splendid for bringing to the table and serving the soup steaming hot as they do in many Continental private homes and hotels, leaving the tureen on the table for guests to serve themselves with second helpings.

When making soups at home an electric blender is a great help in preparing many types of soup, or you can use a vegetable mill, or what the French call a mouli légumes.

Bouillon or stock cubes are very useful to supplement home-made stock, but be careful when adding seasoning to soups made with cubes as they are already well seasoned.

The gravy left from stews and casseroles can also make the basis for a good hot soup, especially if there are a few vegetables left in it. These can either be chopped or the gravy put through the electric blender to make a thick, smooth soup, or thinned down with water and bouillon cubes.

Beef Stock

Not many housewives have the time or the inclination these days to make their own stock, for it cannot be made in a hurry and needs hours of simmering. Then it must be allowed to get cold to enable the fat to be skimmed off. Certainly, if you have a pressure cooker this reduces the cooking time, and details of this are given in the book of instructions which come with your cooker, and which should be followed carefully.

But home-made stock does give a splendid base for all kinds of soups, and I am giving instructions here in the hope that some house-wives will follow them for the benefit of their families.

When buying the soup bones ask the butcher to saw or crack the bones for you. This increases the surface exposed to the water when making the stock, and gives more flavour and richness. Always use cold water, and if you have time soak the bones in cold water for about 30 min before cooking. Add the seasonings and vegetables for the last hour of cooking rather than at the beginning.

For a rich brown stock, heat a little beef dripping in a large saucepan and brown the bones on all sides, then cover them with cold water and bring to the boil, then reduce heat to simmering.

	USA	Imperial	Metric
meaty soup bones	3–4lb	3–4lb	1½–2kg
onions	2	2	2
carrot	2	2	2
celery	1 stalk	1 stalk	1 stalk
bay leaf	1	1	1
parsley	3 sprigs	3 sprigs	3 sprigs
salt and pepper, to taste			
water, to cover			

Wash bones, put into saucepan and cover with cold water. Bring to boil, and skim off any scum which has come to the top, then reduce heat and simmer gently for 2½ hr. Add remainder of ingredients and continue simmering for another hour. Strain stock and allow to cool, then skim off fat just before using.

To Clear Stock: For a good clear consommé it may be necessary to clear the stock. Remove fat from the top of the stock, and measure it into a pan. For each quart of stock (approx 1l) add 1 beaten egg white and the crushed egg shell. Be careful not to include any yolk of egg. Bring stock to boiling point, stirring constantly, and boil for 2 min.

Then reduce heat and stand stock over low heat for 20 min. Strain through muslin or a very fine nylon strainer, and it should be quite clear.

Chicken Stock

If you are cooking a chicken to be used in a fricassée or served whole with a sauce, or in a pie, you will have a good quantity of chicken stock which can be served as a plain chicken consommé at another meal, or as one of the other soups calling for chicken stock in this section.

Most chickens these days are bought frozen, with their giblets tucked in a plastic bag inside them. These giblets add good flavour and body to the stock, so never discard them, but soak them in cold water for $\frac{1}{2}$ hr, clean them up, and put into the pan with the chicken. You can also add $\frac{1}{2}$ bay leaf, 1 carrot, 1 onion, a stalk of celery and a few sprigs of parsley, as well as some salt, and cover the bird with cold water. Bring to the boil and skim off all the scum which will rise to the surface, then simmer the bird for 1$\frac{1}{2}$–2 hr, depending on the age and size, until it is tender.

Remove bird from stock, and strain the stock, then leave to cool and put into refrigerator. The fat will settle on the top and can easily be peeled off. This fat has many uses in cooking so don't throw it away. The stock should be a thick jelly, and can be served as it is for jellied consommé or used as the basis for a number of soups.

Another method of making chicken stock is to use the carcass. I was brought up by a Scottish grandmother who never wasted anything, and she taught me this trick in the days when chickens were only served on Sundays or special occasions.

First, clean the carcass of any stuffing which may have been left, then break it up and put into a saucepan with the cleaned giblets (if they haven't already been used for gravy stock) and the vegetables as given above. Cover with cold water, and follow directions above. This stock will not be as strong as that made from a whole chicken, but it will make a good basic stock for many soups.

The above directions can be used with duck or turkey carcasses when they are available.

Japanese Chicken and Mushroom Soup (serves 6)

As with all Japanese dishes, this soup looks most attractive as a first course.

	USA	Imperial	Metric
chicken	2lb	2lb	800g
salt, to taste			
cornflour (cornstarch)	4 tbsp	2oz	50g
mushrooms	¼lb	¼lb	100g
spring onion, chopped	1 tbsp	1 tbsp	1 tbsp
lemon	1	1	1
cold water	5 cups	2 pints	1·14l

Put chicken into the cold water, with salt to taste and a thin slice of lemon, bring to boil, then simmer, covered, for 45 min. Drain chicken and reserve the liquid, first removing the lemon. Cut chicken into dice, being careful to remove all bones, and toss in the cornflour until well coated. Drop these pieces into a pan of fast-boiling water and cook for 5 min.

While chicken is cooking, slice mushrooms and cook in the chicken stock for 4–5 min. With a slotted spoon, remove mushrooms from stock and divide between 6 warmed soup bowls. Remove chicken pieces with spoon and also divide between the soup bowls. Add spring onion and a slice of lemon to each bowl and cover with hot chicken stock.

French Onion Soup (serves 4)

This is one version of a classic French soup which everybody who has ever visited France will have enjoyed at some time or another. It should be served in a large ovenproof casserole or soup tureen which can safely be put under the grill.

	USA	Imperial	Metric
onions	1¼lb	1¼lb	600g
butter or margarine	4 tbsp	2oz	50g
beef stock (may be made with cubes)	3¾ cups	1½pints	852ml

	USA	Imperial	Metric
salt and pepper, to taste			
thick slices French bread	4	4	4
cheese, grated	4 tbsp	4 tbsp	4 tbsp

Peel onions and slice very thinly. Melt butter or margarine in a saucepan and cook onion slices until a golden brown, but be very careful they do not burn or the flavour will be spoilt. Add stock or water and bouillon cubes, bring to boil, then simmer, covered, for about 30 min. Add salt and pepper to taste.

Cut 4 slices of crusty French bread about ½in (1cm) thick and put them on the bottom of the casserole or soup tureen, pour the onion soup over them, and when the bread floats to the top sprinkle each slice with grated cheese. Put under a pre-heated grill just until the cheese browns slightly and melts, then serve at once.

Pepperpot Soup (serves 6)

This is a good old-fashioned soup full of meat and flavour to warm you up on a cold winter's day. A bowl of this would make a good supper dish when served with thick hunks of crusty bread, and followed by cheese and fruit it would make a meal. If served at the beginning of a meal, it needs a reasonably light dish to follow.

	USA	Imperial	Metric
shin or stewing beef	1lb	1lb	400g
Worcestershire sauce	4 tbsp	4 tbsp	4 tbsp
salt and pepper, to taste			
celery, chopped	3 sticks	3 sticks	3 sticks
onions, chopped	2 large	2 large	2 large
carrots, diced	2 large	2 large	2 large
bouquet garni	1	1	1
tomato purée	2 tbsp	2 tbsp	2 tbsp
macaroni or rice	4 tbsp	4 tbsp	4 tbsp
butter	2 tbsp	1 oz	25g
flour	1 tbsp	1 oz	25g

Cut beef into 1in (2½cm) cubes and place in a bowl with the sauce to marinate for 12 hr in refrigerator or cool place. Turn the meat occasionally in the sauce.

When ready to cook place meat and the sauce in a large saucepan, add water and salt and bring slowly to the boil. Add vegetables, bouquet garni and tomato purée and simmer until meat and vegetables are tender, about 25 min. Add rice or macaroni and simmer for a further 30 min. Remove bouquet garni. Work butter and flour to a paste, divide into 4 and stir each portion into the soup until dissolved. Simmer for 5 min, then serve.

Mushroom Soup Madeira (serves 6)

Madeira is a lovely island, with magnificent scenery, and a wonderful fruit and vegetable market where you can buy a wide variety of tropical fruits such as you never see at home. Also produced there are wines which were known and appreciated centuries ago when the taste for sweeter wines was much more prevalent than it is today. The particular flavour of Madeira wine adds considerably to this mushroom soup.

	USA	Imperial	Metric
mushrooms	½lb	½lb	200g
butter	3 tbsp	3 tbsp	3 tbsp
onion, chopped	1 small	1 small	1 small
green pepper	1 medium	1 medium	1 medium
chicken stock	2¾ pints	3 pints	1·7 l
Madeira wine	2 tbsp	2 tbsp	2 tbsp
lemon slices	3	3	3

Wash mushrooms well. Chop stems and slice mushroom caps. Carefully remove seeds and membranes from green pepper, then chop small. Melt butter in fairly large saucepan and cook onion, green pepper and mushroom stems for 4–5 min. Add mushroom slices and cook for 5 min, stirring occasionally. Add chicken stock and bring to boil, then simmer for a few minutes. Add wine and divide between 6 bowls. Float ½ slice of lemon on each one.

Page 67 (*above*) Gazpacho;
(*right*) pepperpot soup

Page 68 (*above*) Roll mops; (*below*) savoury kipper medley

Mussel Soup (serves 4–5)

This is a delicious soup to make when you can get fresh mussels, which should be prepared as directed on page 109, then added to the vegetable purée.

	USA	Imperial	Metric
mussels	5 cups	2 pints	1·14l
butter	3 tbsp	1½oz	37½g
onion, chopped	1 small	1 small	1 small
celery, chopped	1 stalk	1 stalk	1 stalk
parsley stalks	3–4	3–4	3–4
flour	1 tbsp	1 tbsp	1 tbsp
hot milk	3¾ cups	1¼ pints	850ml
salt and pepper, to taste			
single cream	¼ cup	2 fl oz	56ml
parsley, chopped	2 tsp	2 tsp	2 tsp

Melt butter in a large saucepan, add onion, celery and parsley stalks and cook for a few minutes without colouring. Blend in the flour, cook for 1 min, then gradually stir in milk. Cover and cook gently for 20 min, until vegetables are quite tender. Rub through a sieve, or put through an electric blender, then return to rinsed-out pan.

Have mussels ready prepared, and strain stock through muslin into the above mixture. Add mussels taken from their shells, and bring just to the boil, then add cream and heat but do not boil. Serve with parsley.

Fish Chowder (serves 4–5)

This soup is substantial enough to serve as a meal by itself for supper, followed by a dessert, or I have sometimes doubled the quantities and served it for a buffet meal for 8 people. Use any coarse white fish available, but I find cod makes a good chowder.

	USA	Imperial	Metric
coarse white fish	1lb	1lb	400g
cold water	3 cups	1¼ pints	678ml

	USA	Imperial	Metric
butter or margarine	1 tbsp	1 tbsp	1 tbsp
onion, chopped	1 medium	1 medium	1 medium
garlic (if liked)	1 clove	1 clove	1 clove
carrots, diced	2	2	2
potatoes, diced	2 large	2 large	2 large
celery, diced	2 stalks	2 stalks	2 stalks
flour	2 tsp	2 tsp	2 tsp
milk	2¼ cups	1 pint	568 ml
bay leaf	1	1	1
fresh thyme and tarragon	2–3 sprigs	2–3 sprigs	2–3 sprigs
salt and pepper, to taste			
lemon slices	4–5	4–5	4–5
parsley, chopped, to garnish			

Heat butter in a large saucepan and lightly fry the onion and garlic, then remove garlic. Add water, prepared carrots, potatoes, celery, bay leaf and herbs tied together, then the fish. Cover and bring to the boil, then simmer gently for 20 min. Remove fish and herbs tied together. Carefully flake the fish, removing any dark skin and bones. Blend flour with a little of the milk, then add remainder of the milk to the vegetables in the saucepan and bring to the boil. Stir in blended flour until soup thickens slightly, add flaked fish and re-heat, then pour into heated soup bowls. Garnish each bowl with a slice of lemon dipped in chopped parsley.

For a special occasion a few shelled shrimps could be added with the fish.

Flemish Soup (serves 6)

Make this when Brussels sprouts are in season, particularly if you have them growing in your garden. If you have no chicken stock available make up the required amount with chicken bouillon cubes and water, but be careful of the seasoning.

	USA	Imperial	Metric
Brussels sprouts	1 lb	1 lb	400g
onion, chopped	1 tbsp	1 tbsp	1 tbsp

	USA	Imperial	Metric
butter or margarine	2 tbsp	2 tbsp	2 tbsp
chicken broth	5 cups	2 pints	1·14l
potatoes	2 medium	2 medium	2 medium
hot milk	½ cup	4 fl oz	113ml
salt and pepper, to taste			

Trim the sprouts and wash thoroughly, then pour boiling water over them, stand for 2 min and drain well. Melt butter in a large saucepan and cook sprouts and onion for 3 min turning occasionally. Add potatoes and chicken broth, cover and simmer for 15–20 min, or until the vegetables are tender. Rub through a sieve or put through an electric blender, add milk and re-heat without allowing to boil. Taste for seasoning and serve with croûtons (p 80).

Cream of Vegetable Soup (serves 5–6)
A good soup which needs no stock.

	USA	Imperial	Metric
carrots	2	2	2
parsnip	1	1	1
turnip	1	1	1
potatoes	2	2	2
onion	2	2	2
parsley or celery leaves, chopped	2 tbsp	2 tbsp	2 tbsp
milk	5 cups	2 pints	1·14l
water	1¼ cups	½ pint	284ml
flour	1 heaped tbsp	1 heaped tbsp	1 heaped tbsp
butter	1 tbsp	1 tbsp	1 tbsp
salt and pepper, to taste			

Wash and peel the vegetables, then grate on a coarse grater, except the onion which is sliced thinly. Melt butter in pan and cook the onion until transparent, but do not brown, then add other vegetables

71

and cook, covered, for a few minutes. Add water and simmer for 15 min. Add milk and bring to boiling point. Blend flour with a little milk and stir into soup, stirring until mixture thickens slightly. Taste for seasoning, sprinkle with chopped parsley or celery leaves and serve.

Cream of Chestnut Soup (serves 4–5)

A good winter soup when chestnuts are available, or you can save time by using canned chestnuts, but be sure they are the unsweetened type.

	USA	Imperial	Metric
chestnuts, peeled	1 lb	1 lb	400g
butter or margarine	2 tbsp	1 oz	25g
onion	1	1	1
stock	5 cups	2 pints	1·14l
milk	not quite ¾ cup	¼ pint	141ml
top milk or cream	2 tbsp	2 tbsp	2 tbsp
salt and pepper, to taste			
sugar	½ tsp	½ tsp	½ tsp
lemon rind, grated	1 tsp	1 tsp	1 tsp
paprika, to garnish			

If using fresh chestnuts make a slit in both ends with a sharp knife. Cover with water and boil for about 20 min, then drain and peel. Slice the onion and the chestnuts and fry in the butter or margarine for a few minutes, then add the stock (may be made from chicken stock cubes), cover and simmer until chestnuts are quite tender. Rub through a sieve or put through an electric blender. Add sugar, lemon rind, salt and pepper to taste and milk and re-heat. Divide between soup plates and sprinkle top with paprika.

Cream of Celery Soup (serves 6)

	USA	Imperial	Metric
young celery	1 head	1 head	1 head
medium onion	1	1	1

	USA	Imperial	Metric
potato	1 large	1 large	1 larg.
butter or margarine	1 tbsp	1 tbsp	1 tbsp
chicken stock	5 cups	2 pints	1·14 l
flour	1 tbsp	1 tbsp	1 tbsp
milk	1¼ cups	½ pint	284ml
salt and pepper, to taste			
parsley, chopped	1 tbsp	1 tbsp	1 tbsp
cheese, grated	2 tbsp	2 tbsp	2 tbsp

Wash and cut up celery, including some of the freshest leaves. Slice onion and cube potato. Heat butter in saucepan and cook celery and onion until pale golden. Blend in flour, then stir in stock (may be made from chicken stock cubes), add potato and cook for 20 min, or until vegetables are quite tender. Rub through a sieve or food mill (not a blender), return to saucepan and add milk, parsley, salt and pepper to taste, and re-heat. Serve sprinkled with grated cheese or with croûtons (p 80).

Cream of carrot soup is made in the same way, but substituting 1lb young carrots for the celery. This can be put through an electric blender.

Greek Egg and Lemon Soup (serves 4–6)

This is a very well-known and popular Greek soup, which can be made with home-made chicken stock or with the canned variety, and served either hot or cold.

	USA	Imperial	Metric
canned chicken broth	2 15oz cans	2 15oz cans	2 375g cans
eggs	3	3	3
lemon	1	1	1
lemon rind, grated	1 tsp	1 tsp	1 tsp
pepper, to taste			

Grate the lemon rind, then squeeze out the juice from the lemon. Beat the eggs with the rind and juice. Heat the broth, add some to the eggs and mix well, then add egg mixture to remainder of soup. Heat very gently until egg thickens, but do not allow to boil. If serving hot, taste for seasoning and pour into soup bowls.

If serving cold, allow to cool, then put into refrigerator until chilled. Serve very cold garnished with chopped chives or a lemon slice on each bowl.

This is sometimes served with rice cooked in the chicken broth before adding the eggs, but as the first course for a formal dinner I prefer it without the rice.

Stock made with chicken cubes can also be used.

Chilled Curried Shrimp Soup (serves 4)

This is a splendid soup to make from cans if you should need something rather special to serve in a hurry.

	USA	Imperial	Metric
canned beef consommé	1 15oz can	1 15oz can	1 375g can
curry powder	2 tsp	2 tsp	2 tsp
apple	1	1	1
canned, peeled shrimps	4oz	4oz	100g
single cream	1¼ cups	½ pint	284ml
parsley, chopped	1 tbsp	1 tbsp	1 tbsp
lemon slices	4	4	4

Blend curry powder to a cream with a little of the consommé. Heat remainder of consommé and pour over blended curry, stirring to mix well, then heat until nearly boiling. Chill, then stir in cream. Keep aside 4 of the largest shrimps and chop remainder. Peel, core and chop the apple, add with shrimps to soup, then divide soup between 4 soup bowls. Dip each lemon slice in finely chopped parsley, slit it and hang with a shrimp over side of each bowl.

If preferred, this soup can be heated with all ingredients (except lemon slices) and served hot, but do not allow it to boil. Garnish with the lemon slices.

Chilled Borsch (serves 6)

This famous Russian soup is delicious when served chilled, accompanied by side dishes from which guests help themselves as suits their taste. Plain white bowls look the best for serving this in, if you have them.

	USA	Imperial	Metric
uncooked beetroots	5–6	5–6	5–6
onion, chopped	1	1	1
cooking apple	1	1	1
cabbage, shredded	1½oz	1½oz	37½g
milk	2¼ cups	1 pint	568ml
water or chicken stock	2¼ cups	1 pint	568ml
salt, to taste			
sugar	1 tsp	1 tsp	1 tsp
cream or yoghurt	½ cup	4 fl oz	113ml
lemon juice	1 tsp	1 tsp	1 tsp

As beetroot stains the hands it is advisable to wear rubber gloves while preparing this soup.

Scrub or peel the beetroots as thinly as possible and grate them into a saucepan. Add onion, peeled and chopped apple, cabbage, chicken stock or water with a chicken stock cube and sugar. Bring to the boil and simmer for 1 hr. Strain into a bowl, pressing mixture with the back of a spoon to extract all the juice. Stir in milk and chill until ready to serve. Divide between 6 small soup bowls. Mix cream and lemon juice together and top each bowl with a spoonful of this soured cream, or use yoghurt if preferred.

Side dishes can be flaked crabmeat, chopped hard boiled eggs, chopped cucumber, or caviare. This is the Russian custom, but is not essential except for a very formal dinner.

Hot Borsch (serves 6)

If you prefer to serve this soup hot, which is certainly preferable in winter, follow the above recipe but use all stock (either chicken or beef) instead of stock and milk to make up the quantity of liquid. Instead of straining the soup it can be put through an electric blender.

Chicken and Avocado Soup (serves 4)

This is a very simple soup to make, and it can be served either hot or cold, although I personally consider it better chilled as a summer 'starter'.

	USA	Imperial	Metric
chicken stock	5 cups	2 pints	1·14l
avocado	1 large	1 large	1 large
sherry or lemon juice, to taste			
soured cream or yoghurt, as required			

Make sure the avocado is ripe, then peel it as thinly as possible to keep its green colour. Put into an electric blender with the sherry or lemon juice and 1 cup chicken stock and blend until quite smooth. Mix in remainder of chicken stock and chill until required. Divide between 4 chilled soup cups or bowls, garnish each one with a spoonful of soured cream or plain yoghurt and serve.

If serving hot follow above directions but after blending avocado add it to hot chicken stock and re-heat without allowing to boil. Garnish as above, and sprinkle soured cream with a little paprika for extra colour.

Gazpacho I (serves 8)

This is a famous iced soup found all over Spain. Every city and practically every family has a different version which they swear is the best. From being a peasant soup it has now become a fashionable speciality, served with pride in all the best Spanish restaurants. It must be served very cold, and is usually accompanied by little bowls of 'extras' for each person to help himself to those he prefers.

	USA	Imperial	Metric
garlic	2 cloves	2 cloves	2 cloves
onion	1 large	1 large	1 large
green pepper	1	1	1
ripe tomatoes	6 large	6 large	6 large
cucumber	4in long	4in long	10·16cm long
olive oil	½ cup	4 fl oz	113ml

	USA	Imperial	Metric
red wine vinegar	3 tbsp	3 tbsp	3 tbsp
iced water	6¼ cups	2½ pints	1·42l

Peel the onions, garlic, tomatoes and cucumber, remove seeds and membranes from pepper. If you have an electric blender put all ingredients except water into it and run at low speed for a few seconds. Add iced water, season to taste and serve in chilled bowls.

If you haven't a blender, chop the above ingredients as small as possible, stir in oil gradually, mashing the vegetables with the oil and vinegar, then strain into a deep bowl. Pour in the iced water and season to taste, then serve.

Small bowls of chopped peeled tomato, small cubes of cucumber, diced sweet red pepper, and croûtons (p 80) or toast may be served separately.

Gazpacho II (serves 6)
This is another version of the above recipe.

canned condensed tomato soup	1 large can
water	1 soup can
cucumber, thinly sliced	1 cup
green pepper, chopped	⅓ cup
grated onion	⅓ cup
garlic, pressed	1 clove
olive oil	⅓ cup
wine vinegar	2 tbsp
salt and pepper, to taste	

If you use the same cup for measuring all ingredients the quantities are near enough for this.

Combine all the ingredients, cover and chill for at least 4 hr. Serve in chilled bowls.

Vichyssoise (serves 4–5)
Although often described as a French soup, this iced cream soup actually came from America—but it was created by a famous French chef who was working in a New York hotel. It is fine for a summer meal.

	USA	Imperial	Metric
large leeks	5–6	5–6	5–6
butter or margarine	4 tbsp	2oz	50g
potatoes	4	4	4
chicken stock	5 cups	2 pints	1·14l
salt and pepper, to taste			
ground nutmeg	pinch	pinch	pinch
cream	½ cup	4 fl oz	113ml
chives, chopped, to garnish			

Use only the white part of the leeks, and cut into 1in (2½cm) lengths, washing very well to remove all sand. Sauté in butter or margarine until soft, but do not allow to colour. Peel and slice potatoes and add to leeks with chicken stock and seasonings, then simmer until vegetables are soft. Put through a fine sieve, or an electric blender. Chill overnight, then just before serving stir in cream, and divide between 4 or 5 soup bowls and sprinkle with chopped chives.

This soup can also be served hot if preferred.

Austrian Cold Beef Broth (serves 6)
Whether you use good beef stock as made at home (p 61) or plain beef bouillon cubes is a matter of time and taste, but in Austria most housewives still have a stock pot on their stoves, even in summer. This is a most refreshing start to a meal on hot days.

	USA	Imperial	Metric
beef broth	3¾ pints	3 pints	1·71l
lemon juice	1 tbsp	1 tbsp	1 tbsp
tomatoes	6 small	6 small	6 small
parsley, chopped	1 tbsp	1 tbsp	1 tbsp
salt and pepper, to taste			

The broth should be clear and cold. Add strained lemon juice. Peel tomatoes, cut in halves and squeeze out the seeds, then cut into thin slices. Place these in bottom of soup cups or bowls, sprinkle with a little finely chopped parsley and fill up with cold broth. Chill and serve.

QUICK SOUPS

Canned soups are manufactured in such variety these days that a clever hostess can serve them to her guests without any qualms, especially if she 'dresses them up' before taking to the table. Try some of these garnishes and combinations.

Canned Consommé

Put a can of consommé into the refrigerator overnight, when it will jelly. Divide between 4 small bowls, top each with a spoonful of sour cream, and sprinkle with a very little finely chopped parsley.

OR Shred some carrot and turnip and cook in a little water for 10 min. Drain well. Heat canned consommé and pour over vegetables.

OR Wash button mushrooms and cut into thin slices. Cook in a little water for 5 min, then add consommé and heat.

Asparagus Soup

Using chicken stock cubes, make up enough soup for required number of guests. Drain liquor from a can of asparagus tips into chicken soup; chop the asparagus into pieces and add to soup. Re-heat and serve in bowls or cups. Garnish with lemon slices dipped in finely chopped parsley.

Mushroom and Crab Chowder

Flake a small can of crab, removing any hard membranes. Make up 1 can condensed cream of mushroom soup with 1½ cans milk or milk and water, add flaked crab and heat without allowing to boil.

Other suggestions:

Add a spoonful of whipped cream flavoured with paprika to each bowl of canned chicken, asparagus or tomato soup just before serving.

OR Add grated cheese to vegetable soup, or sprinkle chopped chives over the top. Use scissors to chop the chives.

GARNISHES FOR SOUP

Croûtons are a popular garnish for many different kinds of soup, and they are easy to prepare well in advance of serving. Just cut stale bread into very small dice and fry them in deep hot oil or in a shallow pan of butter until they turn brown and crisp. Drain thoroughly on kitchen paper.

For garlic croûtons fry a peeled, crushed clove of garlic in the butter or oil before frying the bread.

If you have been making pastry the day before, keep some of the left-over pieces in the refrigerator, then cut them into small dice, drop in hot fat or oil until crisp and browned and serve with the soup. They will puff up and look quite attractive.

Fish for
First Courses

When you prefer to commence your meal with fish the choice is very wide, ranging from the almost too popular shrimp cocktail to simpler but tasty herrings.

Many of the recipes given here for fish as a first course could also be adapted quite easily for a main dish by increasing the amounts, and they would also be most appropriate for a buffet party, but it is as a 'starter' that the following recipes are suggested.

You will find that some of them need last-minute cooking and garnishing, and these are only recommended if you have somebody to help you in the kitchen who can attend to things while you welcome your guests.

Recipes for fish pâtés have been included in the section on pâtés on page 52.

Can sizes change frequently, and those given here are the sizes available at the time of writing. Either fresh or frozen fish can be used as available, and in most cases frozen fish need not be thawed out before cooking.

Plaice and Grapefruit Rolls (serves 6)

The tartness of the grapefruit adds new flavour to the fish in this hot 'starter'.

	USA	Imperial	Metric
plaice or whiting fillets	6	6	6
grapefruit	2	2	2
plain flour	¼ cup	1oz	25g
butter or margarine	2 tbsp	1oz	25g
milk	almost 1 pint	¾ pint	426ml
salt and pepper, to taste			
capers	2 tsp	2 tsp	2 tsp
parsley, chopped, to garnish			

Skin the grapefruit and divide them into segments, peeling away the membranes. Remove skin from fish fillets and season with a little salt and pepper. With the skin side uppermost, place a grapefruit segment at the head end of each fillet and roll it up. Place the rolls in a shallow ovenproof dish so they will keep their shape.

Melt butter or margarine in a pan over low heat, remove from heat and stir in flour, then gradually blend in milk. Return to heat and stirring all the time bring sauce to the boil until it thickens. Stir in capers and taste for seasoning. Pour sauce over fish, cover with lid or a piece of foil and bake in a moderate oven (350° F, 180° C, Gas Mark 4) for 25–30 min.

Dip the wide edge of each of the remaining grapefruit segments into the chopped parsley and place on top of the fish dish in a spiral design; serve at once.

Plaice Gouda

Another version of the above dish uses fingers of Gouda cheese instead of grapefruit segments, and the fish fillets are rolled round the cheese, which is seasoned with a few grains of cayenne. After the fish is cooked the top is garnished with slices of tomato and returned to the oven just long enough to heat these.

Or instead of putting tomato slices on top of the dish, thick slices of tomato can be grilled and each fish roll served on a tomato slice, then covered with the sauce.

Baked Fish with Anchovies (serves 6)

Practically any white fish fillets can be used for this dish, but I find either plaice or whiting the most satisfactory.

	USA	Imperial	Metric
plaice fillets	6	6	6
anchovy fillets	8	8	8
soured cream	½ cup	4 fl oz	113ml
pepper, to taste			
browned breadcrumbs	3 tbsp	3 tbsp	3 tbsp
butter	1 tbsp	1 tbsp	1 tbsp
lemon wedges	6	6	6

Remove dark skin from fish, lay the fillets down and beat them gently with the back of a knife to keep them flat. Place fillets in a buttered shallow ovenproof dish. Season with pepper. Chop the anchovies and mix with soured cream and spread this over the fish. Sprinkle with breadcrumbs and dot with pieces of butter. Bake in a moderately hot oven (400° F, 200° C, Gas Mark 6) for about 25–30 min, or until fish is cooked through.
Serve garnished with lemon wedges.

Crab Cocktails Piquante (serves 4)

Attractive-looking cocktails, these can be prepared well ahead of dinner time and left to chill.

	USA	Imperial	Metric
cooked crab	6–8oz	6–8oz	150–200g
lettuce, chopped	4 tbsp	4 tbsp	4 tbsp
mayonnaise (p 119)	2 tbsp	2 tbsp	2 tbsp
sour cream	2 tbsp	2 tbsp	2 tbsp
tomato ketchup	1 tbsp	1 tbsp	1 tbsp
chives, chopped	1 tsp	1 tsp	1 tsp

	USA	Imperial	Metric
gherkins, chopped	¼ tsp	¼ tsp	¼ tsp
capers, chopped	½ tsp	¼ tsp	½ tsp
hard boiled eggs	2	2	2
parsley, chopped	1 tsp	1 tsp	1 tsp

Mix together the mayonnaise, sour cream, ketchup, chives, gherkins, capers and leave to stand for at least an hour in the refrigerator for flavours to blend. Just before dinner shred or chop the lettuce and put some in each of 4 goblets. Divide crabmeat into chunks, removing the hard membranes, and divide between the goblets, then top with mayonnaise mixture. Finely chop the eggs and mix with the parsley and sprinkle cocktails with this.

Serve with fingers of fresh brown bread and butter.

Crab Imperial (serves 6)

Either fresh or canned crabmeat can be used for this special dish with which to start a special dinner. It is cooked in either scallop shells or small ovenproof ramekins.

	USA	Imperial	Metric
crabmeat	1lb	1lb	400g
capers	1 tbsp	1 tbsp	1 tbsp
mayonnaise (p 119)	¼ cup	4 fl oz	113ml
breadcrumbs, dried	¼ cup	2oz	50g
butter, melted	3 tbsp	1¼oz	37½g
salt and pepper, to taste			
lemon rind, grated	1 tsp	1 tsp	1 tsp
paprika, to garnish			

Carefully pick over the crabmeat and remove any hard membranes, then flake and blend with mayonnaise, capers, lemon rind and season to taste. Divide between 6 buttered scallop shells or ramekins. Stir breadcrumbs into the melted butter and cover shells or ramekins, then dust with paprika. Bake in a moderate oven (350° F, 180° C, Gas Mark 4) for about 20 min or until heated through and golden brown on top. Serve on small plates with paper doilies to prevent shells slipping.

Crab Marguerite (serves 4)

Instead of the more usual prawn cocktail, serve this made with canned crab. It has the added advantage that it is slimming as well as tasty.

	USA	Imperial	Metric
crabmeat	2 3½oz cans	2 3½oz cans	175g can
cucumber	4in piece	4in piece	4in piece
parsley, chopped	1 tbsp	1 tbsp	1 tbsp
natural yoghurt	1¼ cups	10 fl oz	284ml
lemon juice	1 tbsp	1 tbsp	1 tbsp
salt and pepper, to taste			
watercress or shredded lettuce, to garnish			

Use 4 stemmed goblets for these if available, and put some watercress or shredded lettuce in the bottom of each glass.

Pick over the crabmeat and remove any hard membranes, then mix crab with chopped and peeled cucumber, yoghurt, lemon juice and parsley and season to taste. Serve on top of watercress or lettuce in glasses. Cut a slice of lemon for each glass, split each one almost in half and hang a slice on the side of each crab cocktail.

Avocado Seafood Cocktail

A mixture of fish such as crabmeat, shelled prawns or tuna can be used for the filling in this tasty 'starter'.

Cut avocados in halves and prepare as described on page 40, but scoop out the pulp, leaving a firm margin all round the skin. Brush over with lemon juice. Mash avocado pulp until smooth (it can be put through an electric blender), adding a little mayonnaise (p 119) if required to get right consistency, then add chopped prawns or shrimps, crabmeat, canned tuna or other fish as available. Season to taste and fill avocado shells. Serve garnished with lemon quarters.

Grapefruit and Seafood Cocktail

Instead of avocados used halved grapefruit, cutting out the pulp and dicing it, then mixing with mayonnaise (*p* 119) and seafood, and replacing in the shell. Serve chilled.

Instead of mayonnaise, used soured cream for a change of flavour.

Avocado with Crab (serves 4)

Be sure the avocados are ripe by rolling them between your hands—they should be quite soft. Either fresh or canned crabmeat can be used for this.

	USA	Imperial	Metric
avocados	2	2	2
crabmeat	¼lb	¼lb	200g
mayonnaise (*p* 119), as required			
lemon juice, as required			
lemon rind, grated	1 tsp	1 tsp	1 tsp
lemon slices	4	4	4

Halve avocados and remove stones, and brush cut part over with lemon juice to prevent discolouring. Pick over the crabmeat and remove any hard membranes, then mix with grated lemon rind and just enough mayonnaise to bind it together without making it soggy. Fill avocado halves and garnish with lemon slices.

If you want these to look really special, serve them on beds of crushed ice.

Crab-Stuffed Mushrooms (serves 8)

These make a really special beginning for a good dinner, and they have the added advantage that they can be prepared well before serving time. But you must be able to obtain 16 large mushroom caps from your greengrocer, ones that are at least 3in (7·62cm) across, so order them well beforehand.

	USA	Imperial	Metric
large mushrooms	16	16	16
crabmeat	4oz	4oz	100g
dried breadcrumbs	4 tbsp	4 tbsp	4 tbsp

	USA	Imperial	Metric
eggs	2	2	2
double cream	2 tbsp	2 tbsp	2 tbsp
parsley, chopped	2 tbsp	2 tbsp	2 tbsp
onion, chopped	1 tbsp	1 tbsp	1 tbsp
lemon juice	1 tbsp	1 tbsp	1 tbsp
butter	2 tbsp	2 tbsp	2 tbsp
salt and pepper, to taste			

Wash mushrooms and cut off stalks, but do not peel them. Melt 1 tbsp butter in a frying pan and sauté mushrooms, hollow side up, for 2 min. Transfer mushrooms to a buttered baking dish large enough to take them in one layer. Sauté the finely chopped onion in the butter remaining in frying pan until transparent. Combine crabmeat (be sure to remove any hard membranes), breadcrumbs, beaten eggs, cream and parsley in a bowl, then add onions with any remaining butter, lemon juice, salt and pepper to taste, and mix all very well together. Fill mushroom caps with this mixture, dot each with a little butter and place in a moderate oven (350° F, 180° C, Gas Mark 4) for about 15 min, until mushrooms are tender and filling cooked through and nicely browned.

These can be served on rounds of fried bread if liked.

If you are living anywhere where oysters are not terribly expensive, omit the crabmeat in the above recipe, place two oysters in each mushroom cap and cover with the filling mixture, then bake as directed. Wonderful.

Crab and Tomato Layers

These look very attractive served on crisp lettuce leaves. Choose large round tomatoes all the same size, allowing 1 tomato for each serving. For a special dinner crabmeat is good for the filling, or use chopped, well-drained anchovies mixed with chopped hard boiled eggs, or chopped sardines instead of the anchovies.

Cut the tomatoes into three equal slices, blend the crabmeat with mayonnaise (p 119) and chopped pickled cucumber and sandwich the tomato slices together again very neatly. Serve on lettuce on individual plates and pass round extra mayonnaise separately.

Shrimps in Orange Cups

For each portion allow 1 orange, 1 hard boiled egg, and 1oz (25g) of peeled shrimps, also salt and pepper and mayonnaise (*p* 119).

Wash oranges and cut a slice from the top of each one. Scoop out the flesh and chop, first removing any seeds and membranes. Chop eggs and mix with orange pulp and peeled shrimps and add just enough mayonnaise to bind mixture together. Taste for seasoning. Fill orange shells with shrimp mixture, replace slice taken from top and chill before serving.

Flaked crab can be used instead of shrimps if preferred.

Coquilles St Jacques à la Bretonne (serves 4-5)

Scallops must have been very popular throughout Europe in medieval times and earlier, for the scallop shell is to be found as a decorative motif in many ancient architectural gems. You can find it in Greek ruins as well as in those of South America dating from long before Christ, yet the scallop shell was adopted as their emblem by Christian pilgrims making their way across Europe to the shrine of St James at Santiago de Compostela in Spain.

The scallop is a delicious bivalve shellfish, looking more like a tropical fish than one which grows in cold waters. It is no wonder its shell found favour with so many artists and architects for it is a delightful fan-shape and most decorative as well as useful. The scallop itself has an orange 'tongue' or coral while the main body of the fish is creamy white. They need little preparation, just remove the black thread, wash and dry them well and trim the edges of the white part just a little (I use the kitchen scissors for this), as this edge becomes hard when cooked. This white part can be sliced into 2 or 3 rounds.

This French way of serving them is probably the best known and certainly makes a delicious first course for dinner. Serve the cooked scallops in their own shells.

	USA	Imperial	Metric
scallops	8	8	8
onion, chopped	1 small	1 small	1 small

	USA	Imperial	Metric
butter	¼ cup	2oz	50g
dry white wine or cider	½ cup	4 fl oz	113ml
parsley, chopped	2 tsp	2 tsp	2 tsp
fresh breadcrumbs	1 tbsp	1 tbsp	1 tbsp
salt and pepper, to taste			
browned breadcrumbs	2 tbsp	2 tbsp	2 tbsp
extra butter, melted	1 tbsp	1 tbsp	1 tbsp

Cut scallops into small dice and put into a pan with the onion and half the butter. Cook gently for a minute then add wine or cider, parsley and fresh crumbs and simmer *very* gently for 6–7 min. Add seasonings and remaining butter in small pieces and leave to melt.

Have ready 4 or 5 deep scallop shells, well buttered, and divide mixture between them. Toss the browned breadcrumbs in the melted butter and sprinkle over the scallops. Put into a hot oven (425° F, 220° C, Gas Mark 7) until crisp and browned on top.

Scallops with Mushrooms (serves 4–5)
Cook the scallops as in above recipe but omit the fresh breadcrumbs and add 4oz (100g) sliced button mushrooms. Make white sauce as directed on page 116, using the liquor drained from the scallops and mushrooms after they are cooked as part of the sauce, and add 2oz (50g) grated cheese.

Put a little of the sauce into each scallop shell, divide the scallops and mushrooms between the shells and cover with remaining sauce. Sprinkle top with a little more grated cheese and brown as in previous recipe.

Scallops Provençale (serves 4–5)
You need someone in the kitchen for these as they must be served as soon as they come from the grill.

	USA	Imperial	Metric
scallops	8	8	8
garlic	1 clove	1 clove	1 clove
butter	½ cup	4oz	100g

	USA	Imperial	Metric
onion, minced	1 tbsp	1 tbsp	1 tbsp
parsley, chopped	1 tbsp	1 tbsp	1 tbsp
salt and pepper, to taste			

Brown the crushed garlic in the butter, then remove. Add onion, parsley and seasoning and cook for 1 min. Cut scallops into 2 or 3 rounds, put into shallow ovenproof dish and pour butter mixture over. Put under hot grill for 3 min, turning once, and continue grilling until pale brown and bubbling.

Seafood Scallops (serves 6)

This is a tasty mixture of fish, tomatoes and mushrooms, served in scallop shells, or small ovenproof ramekins. The scallop shells can be bought from most fishmongers quite cheaply, and they are very useful for a number of fish dishes to be served as starters. Choose shells that are as deep as possible. Wash and scrub them well, and grease before using each time.

	USA	Imperial	Metric
white fish such as cod or haddock	½lb	½lb	200g
canned tomatoes	8oz	8oz	200g
butter or margarine	¼ cup	2oz	50g
medium onion	1	1	1
mushrooms	4oz	4oz	100g
prawns or shrimps, peeled	4oz	4oz	100g
cornflour	2 tsp	2 tsp	2 tsp
Worcestershire sauce	2 tbsp	2 tbsp	2 tbsp
salt and pepper, to taste			
pkt instant potato	3oz	3oz	75g

Drain tomatoes, and poach fish in tomato juice. Peel and chop onion, melt butter in pan and cook onion until transparent. Add sliced mushrooms and prawns or shrimps and cook for 2 min. When fish is cooked through, remove skin and bones and flake it coarsely. Add to mushroom mixture with the juices from the pan and the chopped tomatoes. Blend cornflour with Worcestershire sauce and stir into fish mixture, then bring to boil, stirring gently, until thickened. Season to taste, and spoon mixture into 6 greased scallop shells.

Prepare instant potato as directed on packet, making sure it is quite smooth. Put into a piping bag or cone of thick paper and pipe round the shells. Place on an oven tray and put into a moderate oven (350° F, 180° C, Gas Mark 4) for 15 min until potato is browned on top. Serve at once.

Tuna Scallops

Tuna, salmon or other canned fish can be used to make a simpler version of the above recipe. Flake the fish and add to white sauce (p 116), season well, and fill greased scallop shells. Sprinkle tops with breadcrumbs mixed with grated cheese. Bake in a moderate oven until golden and crisp on top. Serve at once.

Chopped canned pimento can be added to the fish for extra flavour and colour.

Tuna à la King (serves 6–7)

Practically any fish can be used for this recipe, from lobster, crab, shrimps, cod or tuna, and it is very useful that it can be prepared some time before it is to be served, then put into the oven to wait until it is needed. Here I have used tuna, which I think is one of the tastiest of the canned fish.

	USA	Imperial	Metric
butter	3 tbsp	1½oz	37½g
plain flour	6 tbsp	1½oz	37½g
milk	scant 2 cups	¾ pint	426ml
mushrooms	2oz	2oz	50g
canned tuna	2 7oz cans	2 7oz cans	2 175g cans
canned sweetcorn with peppers	12oz can	12oz can	300g can
toast triangles, for garnishing			

Melt butter in a large pan, stir in flour and cook without browning, for 2 min. Remove from heat and stir in milk, then cook slowly, stirring all the time, until sauce comes to the boil and thickens. Simmer for 3 min. Wash and slice mushrooms and add to sauce, then add tuna flaked in large pieces (remove dark skin and bones) and the drained sweetcorn. Season to taste and transfer to an ovenproof casserole which can be brought to the table.

Re-heat, uncovered, in a fairly moderate oven (375° F, 190° C, Gas Mark 5) for 15 min. Garnish round the edge of the casserole with small triangles of toast and serve.

This is a good dish for a buffet party.

Salmon and Cucumber Flan (serves 6)

This is one of those recipes which would make a good addition to a buffet party, as well as being a tasty first course for a summer dinner.

	USA	Imperial	Metric
shortcrust pastry (p 172)	6oz	6oz	150g
salmon or tuna	7½oz can	7½oz can	187½g can
cucumber	4in length	4in length	10cm length
mayonnaise (p 119)	4 tbsp	4 tbsp	4 tbsp
soured cream	5 fl oz	5 fl oz	141ml
gelatine	2 tsp	2 tsp	2 tsp
water	3 tbsp	3 tbsp	3 tbsp
wine vinegar	2 tsp	2 tsp	2 tsp
salt and pepper, to taste			
stuffed olives, for garnishing			

Roll out pastry, line an 8in (20·32cm) flan ring and bake it blind in a hot oven (425° F, 220° C, Gas Mark 7) for 10 min. Remove beans and continue baking for a further 10 min until pastry is cooked.

For the filling flake salmon, removing bones and dark skin. Peel cucumber and cut into small cubes and add to salmon with mayonnaise and soured cream. Dissolve gelatine in water and vinegar over hot water and stir into salmon mixture. Season to taste. Spoon into cooled flan case and chill well. Garnish with sliced stuffed olives.

Marinara Flan (serves 6)

Another good addition to a buffet party table, but it also makes a good beginning to a not-too-substantial dinner party when cut in wedges.

	USA	Imperial	Metric
shortcrust pastry (p 172)	6oz	6oz	150g
salmon or tuna	7½oz can	7½oz can	187½g can
eggs	2	2	2
single cream	5 fl oz	5 fl oz	141ml
onion	¼ small	¼ small	¼ small
Worcestershire sauce	2 tbsp	2 tbsp	2 tbsp
shrimps or prawns, shelled	2oz	2oz	50g
anchovy fillets	2oz can	2oz can	50g can
stuffed olives, for garnish			

Follow directions for flan ring as above, but bake for only 5 min after removing beans.

Flake the salmon in a bowl, removing dark skin and bones, and stir in cream, lightly beaten eggs, chopped onion and sauce. Reserve a few prawns for garnishing and chop remainder and add to mixture. Turn into flan case and bake in moderate oven (350° F, 180° C, Gas Mark 4) for 25 min or until set. Cool. Drain anchovy fillets, cut each one in halves lengthwise, and use to make a lattice pattern on top of flan, then arrange sliced olives and halved prawns in lattice. (See p 136.)

Shrimp Vol-au-Vents

A packet of prepared vol-au-vent cases is very useful in making hot first courses, only needing to be filled with a good white sauce (p 116) to which you have added roughly chopped shrimps and a little sherry, then heated through in a moderate oven.

Alternatively a mixture of chopped mushrooms and chopped shrimps could be used for the filling; or flaked tuna and chopped capers could be added to the sauce for a filling, which should be seasoned well.

Serve on small individual plates covered with paper doilies—this prevents the vol-au-vents from slipping and perhaps causing a messy accident.

Tartelettes d'Écossais (serves 4)

These Scottish Tartlets, as a true Scotsman would call them, were served to me by Tony Murray, head chef of the Royal Lancaster Hotel in London, and he very kindly gave me the recipe for this book. It is something to make for a special occasion.

	USA	Imperial	Metric
shortcrust pastry (p 172) tartlets	4	4	4
smoked salmon slices	8	8	8
Parmesan cheese, grated	¼ cup	2oz	50g
thin white sauce (p 116)	1¼ cups	½ pint	284ml
eggs	4	4	4
asparagus tips	8	8	8
parsley sprigs	4	4	4

Make 4in (10cm) tartlet cases and bake them blind (p 171). Scramble the eggs in the usual way. The slices of salmon should be no wider than 3in (7·5cm) and about 4–5in (10–13cm) long. Lay them flat and put a spoonful of scrambled egg on each slice, then roll them up and fit 2 rolls into each tartlet, putting a layer of sauce into each tartlet first. Cover with more sauce and sprinkle with Parmesan cheese.

Bake the tartlets in a moderate oven (350° F, 180° C, Gas Mark 4) for about 10 min, being careful not to brown the pastry cases too much. Remove from oven, place 2 asparagus tips (the green ones look best) on each and put under a hot grill for 1 min, garnish each with a sprig of parsley and serve.

Croûtes d'Anchois

These are very simple 'starters' which can be prepared some hours before serving.

Cut thin slices of bread into rectangles, cutting off the crusts. Fry these in a mixture of butter and oil until crisp and browned, drain well on kitchen paper and leave until cold. Spread with unsalted butter and arrange a well-drained fillet of anchovy on each. Chop hard boiled eggs and make a border all round anchovy. Season with pepper.

Tuna Tartlets

Make little tartlets with shortcrust pastry (*p* 172). Cover the bottom of each tartlet with mayonnaise (*p* 119) then place on top a thick slice of canned tuna. Garnish with a thin slice of lemon dipped in finely chopped parsley.

Sardine Tartlets

Instead of tuna, fill the tartlets with well-drained sardines mashed with a little mayonnaise (*p* 119) seasoned with a few grains of cayenne. Garnish with lemon slices dipped in finely chopped parsley.

Cucumber Salad Boats (serves 4)

This makes a cool beginning for a summer meal. For a special dinner shelled shrimps can be substituted for the tuna fish.

	USA	Imperial	Metric
canned tuna	7½oz can	7½oz can	187½g
cucumbers	2	2	2
red sweet pepper, chopped	1 tbsp	1 tbsp	1 tbsp
chives, chopped	1 tbsp	1 tbsp	1 tbsp
salt and pepper, to taste			
mayonnaise (*p* 119), as required			
lettuce leaves, to garnish			

Choose evenly shaped young cucumbers. Cut them in halves lengthwise, then in halves crosswise to make 4 equal pieces. Score the skins with a fork then, using a pointed teaspoon, scoop out the seeds to make boat shapes. Sprinkle with salt and pepper and turn upside-down to drain for 15 min.

Drain the tuna and remove any dark skin and bones, then flake finely. Mix with chopped red pepper and chives and just enough mayonnaise to bind together. Fill cucumber boats with this mixture, chill and serve on lettuce leaves.

To carry out the idea of boats, sails can be made with thin slices of orange, then stuck into the boats with wooden picks.

Fish-Filled Tomatoes, Cold (serves 6)

	USA	Imperial	Metric
tomatoes	6	6	6
salmon or tuna	7½oz can	7½oz can	187½g
celery, chopped	3 tbsp	3 tbsp	3 tbsp
onion, grated	1 tbsp	1 tbsp	1 tbsp
mayonnaise (p 119), as required			
cucumber, sliced, to garnish			
salt and pepper, to taste			

Choose 6 round tomatoes, all the same (medium) size. Cut a slice from the top of each and carefully scoop out the inside pulp with a teaspoon. Care must be taken not to pierce the outside skin. Season insides with salt and pepper and turn upside-down to drain while you make the filling.

Drain fish and remove any dark skin and bones, then flake. Mix with celery and onion and just enough mayonnaise to bind mixture together without being soggy. Fill tomatoes with this mixture, replace top slices, chill until ready to serve, garnished with cucumber slices.

Any other fish may be used, such as canned crab or shelled shrimps.

Fish-Filled Tomatoes, Hot (serves 6)

You need 1 large, round tomato and 1 fillet of plaice for each serving, also chopped parsley, salt, pepper and butter. These look nice if cooked in small ovenproof ramekins if they are available, or use an ovenproof dish just large enough to keep the tomatoes upright as they bake.

Either fresh or frozen fillets can be used, but if frozen the fish should be thawed before use.

Prepare tomatoes as directed above. Sprinkle each fillet with chopped parsley, salt and pepper and roll up to fit inside a hollowed-out tomato. Add a small piece of butter on top of each tomato. Place each filled tomato in a buttered ramekin and bake in a moderate oven (350° F, 180° C, Gas Mark 4) for 15–20 min until fish is cooked. Be careful not to overcook or the tomatoes may split, which spoils their appearance. If baking all the filled tomatoes in one dish, add 1 tbsp water to the dish. Serve each tomato on a round of fried bread.

Honolulu Pineapple Salad (serves 6)

For those who like a mixture of fish and fruit this is an attractive starter for a special dinner. Choose a large ripe pineapple with a good crown of leaves. The filling can be prepared ahead of time and left in the refrigerator to chill, then the whole dish is assembled just before serving.

	USA	Imperial	Metric
pineapple	1 large	1 large	1 large
cottage cheese	1 cup	8 fl oz	226ml
mayonnaise (p 119)	1 cup	8 fl oz	226ml
sweet red pepper	1 medium	1 medium	1 medium
shrimps, peeled	4–6oz	4–6oz	100–150g
ripe tomatoes	2	2	2
stuffed olives	6	6	6

Cut pineapple in halves lengthwise, cutting right through the leaves, which should have been wiped over beforehand. Carefully cut out the pulp, being careful not to pierce the skin. I find a curved grapefruit knife is good for this. Remove core and eyes from the pineapple pulp, and cut into cubes.

Cut top from red pepper and remove seeds and membranes, then cut into thin strips about 1in (2½cm) long. Peel tomatoes and squeeze out seeds, then cut into small dice. If shrimps are large cut into pieces.

Mix cottage cheese and mayonnaise, then add pineapple cubes, red pepper strips, shrimps, and tomatoes. Season to taste, and chill until ready to serve. Wrap pineapple halves in foil or polythene bags and chill at the same time.

When ready to serve fill pineapple halves with mixture and garnish with sliced stuffed olives. Arrange on serving plate with leaves at alternate ends.

Pass round extra mayonnaise separately.

Pears with Prawns (serves 6)

Several unusual flavours blend well together in this delicious first course for a summer meal.

	USA	Imperial	Metric
canned pear halves	6	6	6
cottage cheese	8oz	8oz	200g
prawns or shrimps, shelled	4oz	4oz	100g
chives, chopped	1 tsp	1 tsp	1 tsp
pepper, to taste			
lettuce cups, as required			

Drain pear halves well, and arrange in lettuce cups on individual plates. Chop prawns roughly and blend into cottage cheese with the chives and season to taste with pepper. Pile mixture into each pear half and serve at once.

Crabmeat can be used instead of prawns if preferred.

Shrimp Croquettes (serves 6)

Oostduinkerke, on the Belgian Channel coast, has a splendid beach which attracts many holidaymakers in the summer. But it has another attraction: it is here that the last of the horse-back shrimp fishermen are to be found. These men, clad in bright yellow oilskins, ride their well-trained horses up and down in the water dragging heavy nets to catch the shrimps, which find plenty of feed here. Every July they have a Shrimp Festival, with parades and stalls selling shrimps cooked in a variety of ways.

The most popular are these Croquettes de Crevettes, which are also a popular dish all over Belgium, and make a tasty first course for a dinner party. It is best not to keep them waiting after cooking, so if you cannot depend on the punctuality of your guests do not plan these unless you have help in the kitchen.

	USA	Imperial	Metric
butter	¼ cup	2oz	50g
flour	½ cup	2oz	50g

	USA	Imperial	Metric
milk or fish stock	1¼ cup	½ pint	284ml
cooked and chopped shrimps	6oz	6oz	150g
cayenne pepper, a few grains			
salt and pepper, to taste			
egg	1	1	1
double cream	2 tbsp	2 tbsp	2 tbsp
flour, as required			
breadcrumbs, browned, as required			
deep, hot fat or oil, as required			

Melt butter in a thick pan. Sprinkle in the flour and cook until frothy, without colouring it. Remove from heat and stir in milk or stock, then stir over low heat until flour is cooked. Add shrimps, cayenne and seasoning to taste and cook for a minute, then stir in egg yolk beaten with the cream.

Turn the mixture out on to a plate and leave until quite cold, then cut into small pieces and form into cork-shaped croquettes. Roll in the flour, and brush off any excess, then dip in the beaten egg white and then into the fine browned breadcrumbs, coating them well on all sides. Fry croquettes, 2 or 3 at a time, in the deep fat or oil until golden brown, drain on crumpled kitchen paper, and serve hot.

A good accompaniment is fried parsley sprigs, which are fried until crisp in the same fat or oil and drained well.

For a buffet party, make the croquettes smaller and impale each one on a cocktail stick.

Tuscany Beans and Tuna (serves 6–8)

This was once a peasant dish as served in the Tuscany province of Italy, but it can now be enjoyed in many of the most fashionable restaurants of Rome, under the name of Fagioli Toscana col Tonno. Use good-quality white haricot beans or the larger butter beans, which need to be soaked overnight before cooking.

You can use canned butter beans, but I prefer to cook my own.

	USA	Imperial	Metric
dried white beans	2 cups	1 lb	400g
garlic (if liked)	1 clove	1 clove	1 clove
salt	2 tsp	2 tsp	2 tsp
onion rings	3 tbsp	3 tbsp	3 tbsp
French dressing (p 122)	¼ cup	4 fl oz	113ml
canned tuna	2 7oz cans	2 7oz cans	2 175g cans
parsley, finely chopped	1 tbsp	1 tbsp	1 tbsp

Wash the beans, then soak in water overnight, or at least for 4–6 hr, then cook slowly in the same water with peeled clove of garlic and bay leaf until tender (about 2 hr), adding the salt about halfway through cooking time. Drain well and discard garlic, then spread out on clean tea towel to dry. Pour boiling water over onion rings and stand for 10 min, then drain well. Toss beans with onion and French dressing, then the flaked tuna, and divide between 6 serving plates. Sprinkle with parsley.

Portuguese Tomatoes (serves 6)

Many tons of sardines are caught off the coast of Portugal, and at night you can see the women sitting on the beach waiting for the fishing boats to come in. They help unload them and the fish go direct to the canneries, and a loud siren is blown to notify the cannery workers that their services are required at once—so you can see the sardines you buy are very freshly canned. This is one way of using them.

	USA	Imperial	Metric
tomatoes	6	6	6
hard boiled eggs	2	2	2
sardines	2 3½oz cans	2 3½oz cans	2 87½g cans
mayonnaise (p 119), as required			
capers, chopped	1 tbsp	1 tbsp	1 tbsp
salt and pepper, to taste			

Choose round tomatoes all the same size. Cut a thin slice from the end of each tomato and scoop out the pulp. Sprinkle insides with salt and pepper and turn upside-down to drain while you make filling. Drain the sardines and chop them. Shell eggs and chop, keeping one yolk aside. Mix with sardines and capers and bind with a little mayonnaise. Fill tomato cases and chill until ready to serve. Chop egg yolk and sprinkle a little on each tomato top.

Grapefruit Soused Herrings (serves 4)
This is a tasty combination of herrings and fruit, this time grapefruit.

	USA	Imperial	Metric
herrings	4	4	4
onion	1	1	1
mixed pickling spice	2 tsp	2 tsp	2 tsp
grapefruit	2	2	2
vinegar	½ cup	4 fl oz	113ml
salt	1 tsp	1 tsp	1 tsp
sugar	1 tsp	1 tsp	1 tsp
bay leaf	1	1	1
tomatoes	2 large	2 large	2 large
pickled cucumber, as required			

Clean and bone herrings, removing the heads, and cut into fillets. Roll up each fillet, skin inwards and starting from the head, and fasten with wooden picks or tie with cotton. Arrange in an ovenproof dish. Cover with onion rings. Wash grapefruit, cut in halves and squeeze out the juice, but retain the skins. Mix juice with vinegar, pickling spice, salt and sugar and pour over herrings. Add bay leaf. Cover dish and cook in slow oven (300° F, 150° C, Gas Mark 2) for 1½ hr. Cool completely in liquid.

To serve, line grapefruit shells with small lettuce leaves, place a herring roll in each (don't forget to remove cotton or pick) and garnish with tomato quarters and fingers of pickled cucumber.

Serve with tartare sauce (*p* 120) or mayonnaise (*p* 119).

Herrings Smetana (serves 6)
This is a Polish version of the soused herrings.

	USA	Imperial	Metric
soused herrings	6	6	6
soured cream	½ cup	4 fl oz	113ml
hard boiled eggs	3	3	3
French mustard	1 tsp	1 tsp	1 tsp
parsley or fennel, chopped, to garnish			

Prepare herrings as directed on page 103, drain well and keep some of the pickling liquor. Arrange herrings on a flat serving dish. Make sauce by blending sieved egg yolks with mustard and sour cream and adding just enough pickling liquor to make a good sauce. Season to taste and pour over herrings. Garnish with parsley or fennel if available.

Soused Herrings with Orange Dressing (serves 6)
The bland, orange-flavoured mayonnaise makes a good contrast to the sharpness of the herrings. Prepare these days before serving and store in refrigerator.

	USA	Imperial	Metric
fresh herrings	6	6	6
malt vinegar	1¼ cups	½ pint	284ml
water	10 tbsp	¼ pint	141ml
mixed pickling spice	1 tbsp	1 tbsp	1 tbsp
bay leaves	4	4	4
small onions	2	2	2
salt and peppercorns, to taste			
large orange	1	1	1
mayonnaise (p 119)	¾ cup	6 fl oz	170ml
lettuce, to garnish			

Scale, bone and clean herrings, and cut into fillets. Season well with salt and pepper and roll up the fillets, skin inwards, from the tail end. Pack these neatly and fairly close together in an ovenproof dish, sprinkle with pickling spice and peppercorns, bay leaves and onions cut into rings. Combine vinegar and water and pour over fish. Cover with lid or cooking foil and bake in a slow oven (300° F, 150° C, Gas Mark 2) for 1½ hr.

Remove from oven and allow fish to cool in the liquid overnight. When ready to serve, drain herrings, retaining only the onion rings.

Wipe orange and grate the rind, being careful not to grate into the white pith. Add rind to the mayonnaise some hours before serving. Cut the orange into dice. Arrange herring rolls on lettuce leaves and garnish with onion rings from the vinegar mixture and the orange pieces. Serve orange mayonnaise separately.

Roll Mops (serves 6)

These are popular in both Germany and the Scandinavian countries, and they make a good addition to a buffet table, or smörgåsbord.

	USA	Imperial	Metric
herrings	6	6	6
salt	4 tbsp	2oz	50g
water	2¼ cups	1 pint	568ml
vinegar	2¼ cups	1 pint	568ml
mixed pickling spice	1 tbsp	1 tbsp	1 tbsp
onion	1 small	1 small	1 small
bay leaf	1	1	1
whole peppercorns	4–6	4–6	4–6

The herrings should be cleaned and boned, then soaked in a brine made with the salt and water for 2 hr.

Prepare the spiced vinegar by adding the pickling spice to the vinegar (white vinegar if available) and slowly bring to the boil. Remove from heat and allow to cool, then strain. Roll up herrings, skin side outwards, adding a few onion rings with each herring. Pack into a wide-necked jar, add bay leaf and cover with spiced vinegar. Cover jar and leave for 5–6 days in a cool place (not the refrigerator).

Trout in Foil

Allow 1 small trout, 1 tbsp melted butter, 2 tbsp chopped mushrooms, 1 tsp chopped parsley, salt and pepper to taste, for each serving. Also rectangles of foil about 18in × 10in (45cm × 25cm), brushed over with butter on the dull side.

Clean trout, place each one in centre of foil rectangle, cover with mushrooms and parsley, season to taste and dribble butter over the top. Fold foil across the top fairly loosely, then fold ends securely. Place foil parcels on flat baking sheet and bake in moderate oven (350° F, 180° C, Gas Mark 4) for about 20–25 min, depending on size of fish.

Serve still in their foil parcels.

Plaice or whiting fillets can also be prepared and cooked like this.

Cold Trout with Cucumber Sauce (serves 4)

This is an unusual way of serving trout as a 'starter' which I first enjoyed in Denmark.

	USA	Imperial	Metric
rainbow trout	4 small	4 small	4 small
lemon	1	1	1
bay leaf	1	1	1
parsley and thyme	2 sprigs	2 sprigs	2 sprigs
peppercorns	3–4	3–4	3–4
onion	2 slices	2 slices	2 slices
carrot	2 slices	2 slices	2 slices
cucumber	4in piece	4in piece	10·16cm piece
plain yoghurt	½ cup	4 fl oz	113ml
salt and pepper, to taste			

Clean the trout but leave the heads on and trim the tails. Wash them well. Cut a slice from the lemon and put into a shallow pan with onion, carrot, bay leaf, parsley and thyme, peppercorns and water to a depth of 1½in. Bring to the boil and simmer for 3–4 min. Add trout and poach gently for 5 min, then remove pan from heat and allow fish to cool in the stock.

To make the sauce peel and finely dice the cucumber. Put into a shallow dish and sprinkle with salt, cover with a plate and leave to stand for 20 min. Drain off excess liquid from cucumber and stir into yoghurt, season to taste, and chill for a little time.

When trout are quite cold remove them very carefully from the pan, drain and arrange on a serving dish. Cut remainder of lemon into thick slices and use to garnish the fish. Serve sauce separately.

Don't put fish into the refrigerator unless absolutely essential as they lose their flavour if too cold.

Salmon and Cucumber Loaf (serves 4–5)
This is simpler to make if an electric blender is used, but this is not essential. Best made in the morning if being served for dinner at night, but for a summer luncheon it can be made the night before.

	USA	Imperial	Metric
mayonnaise (p 119)	¼ cup	2 fl oz	56ml
lemon juice	1 tbsp	1 tbsp	1 tbsp
Worcestershire sauce	2 tsp	2 tsp	2 tsp
gelatine	½oz	½oz	12½g
canned salmon	7¾oz	7¾oz	194½g
celery, chopped	1 stick	1 stick	1 stick
onion, chopped	1 tbsp	1 tbsp	1 tbsp
salt and pepper, to taste			
cucumber, 1 medium			
canned pimento, to garnish			

Turn the salmon out of the can and remove dark skin and bones. Put into blender with mayonnaise, sauce, celery and onion and blend until smooth. Dissolve gelatine in lemon juice and 1 tbsp water, add to blender and blend again. Turn into a loaf tin which has been lined with foil or greaseproof paper with overlapping sides to make it easier to remove loaf when set. Chill until just before serving, then turn out on a chilled plate. Leave cucumber unpeeled and score down sides with a sharp-pointed fork, then cut in ⅛in (⅓cm) slices. Cut pimento into thin strips. Press cucumber slices round sides of the salmon loaf, using a little mayonnaise to stick if necessary, and garnish top with strips of pimento.

Cut in slices to serve.

Canned tuna can be used instead of salmon if preferred.

Tuna Ring with Raita Sauce (serves 6)

You need a ring mould for this mixture of rice and fish, or alternatively, the mixture can be packed into 6 oiled custard cups and turned out on small individual plates and the raita handed round separately. Make it some hours before serving.

	USA	*Imperial*	*Metric*
canned tuna	*12oz can*	*12oz can*	*300g can*
rice, long grain	*¼lb*	*4oz*	*100g*
celery, diced	*4 tbsp*	*4 tbsp*	*4 tbsp*
salt and pepper, to taste			
cucumber	*1 medium*	*1 medium*	*1 medium*
plain yoghurt	*½ cup*	*4 fl oz*	*113ml*
onion, grated	*1 tbsp*	*1 tbsp*	*1 tbsp*
lemon juice	*1 tbsp*	*1 tbsp*	*1 tbsp*
cayenne, few grains			

Cook well-washed rice in plenty of boiling salted water for 12–15 min, or until just tender. Drain and rinse under running hot water, then drain again. Drain tuna (retaining 1 tbsp oil), remove any dark skin and bones, then flake with the oil. Mix with the rice, celery and onion and season to taste, then pack into lightly oiled ring mould. Chill until ready to serve.

Make raita by dicing the peeled cucumber, put into a colander or strainer and sprinkle with salt, then leave to drain for 15–20 min. When drained mix with yoghurt, lemon juice and season with salt and pepper, but remember that cucumber is already salted.

When ready to serve turn tuna and rice mould on to a serving plate and fill centre of mould with raita.

Fish Mousse (serves 4–5)

I have a mould in the shape of a fish which I use to set this mousse in, but it will taste just as good if made in a plain basin mould and garnished with tomato and cucmber slices for extra colour.

	USA	Imperial	Metric
plaice fillets	¾lb	¾lb	300g
lemon juice	1 tsp	1 tsp	1 tsp
tomato ketchup	1 tbsp	1 tbsp	1 tbsp
mayonnaise (p 119)	1¼ cups	½ pint	284ml
Worcestershire sauce	2 tsp	2 tsp	2 tsp
canned pimento, chopped	1 tbsp	1 tbsp	1 tbsp
whipping cream	½ cup	4 fl oz	113ml
egg white	1	1	1
gelatine	½oz	½oz	12½g
bay leaf	½	½	½
parsley	2 sprigs	2 sprigs	2 sprigs
salt and pepper, to taste			

Poach fish fillets in a little salted water with bay leaf, parsley and lemon juice. Drain well, retaining some of the fish stock, and cool. Remove any dark skin and bones and flake with a fork. Dissolve gelatine in 1 tbsp fish stock. Mix fish with tomato ketchup, mayonnaise, sauce, chopped pimento and dissolved gelatine, and mix all well together. Whip cream until thick and fold into mixture, then whip egg white with a pinch of salt and pepper until stiff and fold into fish. Pour into mould and chill until set.

When ready to serve turn out on to a chilled serving plate and garnish with alternate slices of tomato and cucumber.

Instead of plaice use a large can of tuna or salmon. Use peeled shrimps as a garnish.

Cucumber and Tuna Mould (serves 6)

Use a ring mould to set this dish, which can be made the day before serving and kept in the refrigerator.

MOULES MARINIÈRE (MUSSELS)

	USA	Imperial	Metric
large cucumber	1	1	1
gelatine	½oz	½oz	12½g
sugar	2 tsp	2 tsp	2 tsp
salt	1 tsp	1 tsp	1 tsp
lemon juice	1 tbsp	1 tbsp	1 tbsp
white wine			
vinegar	2 tbsp	2 tbsp	2 tbsp
water	1¼ cups	½ pint	284ml
canned tuna	7oz	7oz	175g
mayonnaise (p 119),			
as needed			
tomatoes, large	2	2	2

Peel and slice cucumber thinly and spread out on a plate. Sprinkle with salt and leave to drain for about 20 min. Combine gelatine, sugar and water in pan and heat gently until gelatine has dissolved. Remove from heat and add lemon juice and vinegar and leave until cool but not set. Pour a thin layer of jelly into ring mould and chill until set. Over this arrange a layer of well-drained sliced cucumber, cover with another layer of jelly and chill until set. Repeat these layers until all the cucumber slices are used up, finishing with a layer of jelly. Chill until ready to serve.

Flake the tuna, removing any skin and bones. Peel tomatoes (drop into boiling water for a few minutes and the skin will come off), squeeze them gently to remove seeds, then chop flesh and add to tuna. Add just enough thick mayonnaise to bind this mixture together, seasoning to taste. Chill.

Have a chilled serving plate ready for the mould. Dip mould in hot water for a second or two and turn it out on the chilled plate, then fill centre with tuna mixture. Serve at once.

Instead of mayonnaise use soured cream for a change.

Moules Marinière (Mussels)

I remember many years ago, when we were living in Australia, a friend of my husband's who was an enthusiastic fisherman coming in

MOULES MARINIÈRE (MUSSELS)

with an enormous sackful of mussels he had gathered off the rocks on one of our ocean beaches.

I was staggered—I had never seen so many of the things before, and didn't know what to do with them. I hadn't a saucepan large enough to take more than we could eat at one meal; I begged the neighbours to take more than their share, and finally finished up paying the garbage man to remove those which were left.

But we certainly enjoyed our Moules Marinière, and the mussel soup I made next day (*see p 69*), and I am sure no mussels I have tasted since have had the flavour of those Bass Strait mussels of so long ago. Today I have to go to enormous trouble to obtain even a gallon of mussels, which seems to be the usual measurement, and gives a first course for 4–6 people, depending on your appetite and what is to follow. And if that seems a lot of mussels, remember that there is a lot of shell to get through before you reach the delectable mussels inside.

When you bring the mussels home put them into a large bowl of slightly salted water and leave them for 15 min. Put your hand in and swirl the water round, and any shells which remain open after that should be discarded, as should those with badly broken shells. With a sharp knife scrape off all the barnacles and pull off the little hairy beards, and put back into fresh water until you are ready to cook them.

	USA	Imperial	Metric
mussels, cleaned and prepared as above			
onion, chopped	1 small	1 small	1 small
garlic (if liked)	1 clove	1 clove	1 clove
bay leaf	½	½	½
white wine or lemon juice	¼ cup	2 fl oz	56ml
salt and pepper, to taste			
butter	2 tbsp	1oz	25g
parsley, chopped	2 tbsp	2 tbsp	2 tbsp

Put all ingredients except mussels and parsley into a large pan with a well-fitting lid. Bring to a good boil and drop all the well-drained mussels in at once. Cover tightly and keep heat high for 5 min, shaking pan occasionally. Take a quick look and if mussels have opened they are ready, or if some are opened and others not quite cooked, remove the opened ones with a slotted spoon and continue cooking remainder for another minute.

Divide the mussels, still in their shells, between required number of deep soup plates. Drain the stock in the pan through a piece of muslin to get rid of the sand or grit which may be there. Add chopped parsley and pour stock over mussels.

Serve with plenty of crusty French bread cut in thick slices with which to mop up the tasty gravy—and finger bowls would be a good idea, too.

Moules Ravigote (serves 6–8)

Prepare mussels as in above recipe, only they are removed from the pan and cooled, and one half of each shell is discarded, leaving mussels in the remaining half.

Strain stock as above, then boil quickly until reduced to half. Cool and mix with thick mayonnaise (p 119) and a little anchovy paste or finely chopped anchovies, and coat each mussel with this mixture. Chill before serving.

Savoury Mackerel (serves 4)

Use canned mackerel for this simple 'starter' which can be prepared ahead of time, then heated just before serving.

	USA	Imperial	Metric
canned mackerel	7oz can	7oz can	175g can
mayonnaise (p 119)	1 tbsp	1 tbsp	1 tbsp
Worcestershire sauce	1 tsp	1 tsp	1 tsp
mustard pickle	1 tbsp	1 tbsp	1 tbsp
pepper, to taste			
large slices toast, buttered	2	2	2

Remove dark skin and bones from fish, and drain away excess oil. Chop pickle very small, and mix with mayonnaise and sauce, then mix in flaked fish. Spread on slices of toast, sprinkle with pepper. When

ready to serve, put under hot grill for a few minutes until heated
through and bubbling.

Cut each slice in halves, then in halves again to make 2 fingers for
each serving. Garnish with a ¼ slice of lemon or a sprig of parsley.

Savoury Kipper Medley (serves 6)

Smoked kipper fillets give a piquant flavour to this 'starter' of rice
combined with mushrooms. For a very savoury buffet party dish
double the quantities.

	USA	Imperial	Metric
kipper fillets	15oz	15oz	375g
rice, long-grain	1 cup	7oz	175g
sweet red pepper	1	1	1
celery	4 sticks	4 sticks	4 sticks
button mushrooms	¼ cup	2oz	50g
parsley, chopped	1 tbsp	1 tbsp	1 tbsp

Poach the kipper fillets, drain and skin them, then cut into 1in
pieces. Cook the rice in salted water, drain well and spread out to cool.
Remove seeds from red pepper and chop into dice, chop the celery and
slice the well-washed mushrooms. Combine all ingredients together,
mixing well and put into a serving bowl. Just before serving fold
sauce vinaigrette (p 122) through the mixture.

Simple Smörgåsbord or Buffet Table

Smörgåsbord or koldte bord are the Scandinavian words for what we would call a buffet party, and nobody really arranges these better than the Scandinavians, who have marvellous ways of mixing various kinds of foods, from fish to reindeer meat, so that they look and taste their best.

The Danes are also renowned for their smørrebrød, a word meaning buttered bread, but the Danes aren't content just to make it that simple, and they put all manner of delicious foods on top of the bread and butter to make their Danwiches, or open sandwiches. These are ideal for buffet parties, and you can please yourself how extravagant you are with the toppings—ranging from Danish cheese and herrings to smoked salmon and caviare. You can use various kinds of bread and make toppings combining slices of pork garnished with an orange slice and a prune, or simple slices of salami sausage garnished with raw onion rings. You can use pickled herrings on rye bread, or prawns with mayonnaise, tiny stuffed tomatoes, or liver pâté with fried mushrooms; in fact the choice is almost limitless.

Cold sliced meats—not the paper-thin slices we usually get in the stores, but good slices from big joints, accompanied by salads of all kinds—are a speciality of smörgåsbord, along with a variety of canned fish, most of them left in their cans for guests to help themselves, as well as freshly cooked fish and shellfish; but away from Scandinavia it is not essential that you follow their lead in food so lavishly.

If your buffet party is in winter, start off with a big tureen of soup, such as Pepperpot Soup on page 65, which is guaranteed to warm the party up.

There are tasty sausages available which can be sliced ready for guests to help themselves, and several cooked chickens cut into serving-size pieces are always welcome. Or make two or three Cheese Tarts (p 210), several plates of Stuffed Eggs (p 32) or Stuffed Tomatoes (p 34), and you can be sure your guests will eat well.

CHEESE AND WINE PARTY

If you prefer the simpler preparations of a cheese and wine party these are always enjoyed by your friends if you provide a good assortment of cheeses, an interesting supply of breads and biscuits to go with the cheese, and bowls of salad greens such as lettuce, endive, celery and watercress, garnished with tomatoes and cucumber, carrot sticks and fingers of pickled cucumber.

Cut the bread in thick slices and serve in shallow baskets; cut the butter in cubes and place in small dishes round the table, and be sure there is enough.

The cheese looks good cut in big wedges and arranged on cheese boards, or bring out your bread board if necessary. It is a good idea to label the cheese so everybody knows exactly what they are eating. For details of various cheeses see pages 213–15.

Nobody expects vintage wine at a cheese and wine party, but you should have a choice of white, red and rosé, which can be bought in assorted lots or in gallon flagons.

Here are some suggestions for the quantities required for a party of 20 people.

Cheese: Allow at least 5lb assorted cheeses, which gives ¼lb per person.

Bread and Biscuits: 5 French loaves, cut diagonally in slices; 1lb plain crackers; 1lb cheese-flavoured crackers; 2lb butter cut in cubes.

Wine: 10 bottles assorted wines (1 bottle gives 6 glasses). Or 8l bottles of wine (1 bottle gives 8 glasses). Or ½gall flagons, which will serve 20 glasses. Your wine merchant will help you choose the best assortment for your party.

Salad Dressings & Sauces

As this book contains very few dishes which require a sauce, with the exception of some of the fish dishes, and the puddings—which have a section for sweet sauces all to themselves—I am not giving you a long list of sauce recipes. Basic sauces which can add extra flavour to fish are included, along with a number of mayonnaise variations and salad dressings which you may find useful in making changes with the salads given here to serve as 'starters'.

We are not really a sauce-loving nation, unlike the Continentals who serve a vast array of sauces, and whose sauciers or sauce-chefs are rated very highly indeed for the flavour and smoothness of their products. There are many dishes which are truly enhanced by a good sauce, and it is worth learning how to make these.

Home-made mayonnaise has a flavour entirely different from that bought in a bottle, but even bought mayonnaise can be given an extra piquancy which adds to its flavouring over a number of different salads if you add some seasoning to please your own taste.

White Sauce

This is a good coating sauce, which can be used as it is, or have different flavourings added to suit the food with which it is being served.

	USA	Imperial	Metric
butter or margarine	2 tbsp	1oz	25g
flour	¼cup	1oz	25g
milk	1¼ cups	½ pint	284ml
salt and pepper, to taste			

Heat butter or margarine in a thick pan, remove from heat and stir in flour until smooth, return to heat and cook gently for a few minutes without allowing the mixture, or 'roux' as it is called, to brown. Blend in cold milk, stirring all the time with a wooden spoon, and cook until mixture comes to the boil and mixture is smooth. Cook for 2–3 min, and season to taste.

If mixture should become lumpy, remove from heat and beat it well, or tip mixture into an electric blender and blend until smooth, then return to pan and heat.

Quick Hollandaise: Make the sauce as above, then remove from heat. Whisk in 1 egg and 2 tsp lemon juice or white vinegar. Cook slowly for 2–3 min without allowing to come to the boil.

Cheese Sauce: After sauce has thickened add 2–4oz (50–100g) grated cheese, a little mustard and Worcestershire sauce to taste, and stir over low heat until cheese has melted.

Egg Sauce: After sauce has thickened add 2 hard boiled eggs, chopped small, and a little mustard.

Anchovy Sauce: Add 1 tsp anchovy essence or chopped canned anchovies and a few grains of cayenne. This is good over plain fish.

Mushroom Sauce: Another sauce to serve over fish is made by adding 2–3oz (50–75g) thinly sliced mushrooms which have been cooked in a little butter.

Tomato and Olive Sauce: This can be poured over halved hard boiled eggs to make a 'starter', or over plain white fish. Peel tomatoes and squeeze out the seeds, then chop the flesh. Remove stones from black

Page 118 Danish open
sandwiches

olives and cut flesh into slivers. Add with chopped tomatoes to sauce after it has thickened.

Sweet-Sour Sauce (serves 4–5)

Ideal to serve over plain grilled or poached fish, or over ham rolls for a 'starter'.

	USA	Imperial	Metric
onion	1 large	1 large	1 large
carrot	1	1	1
celery	1 stalk	1 stalk	1 stalk
sugar	1½ tbsp	1½ tbsp	1½ tbsp
stock	1 cup	8 fl oz	226ml
white vinegar	½ cup	4 fl oz	113ml
cornflour	1 tbsp	1 tbsp	1 tbsp
garlic (if liked)	1 clove	1 clove	1 clove
parsley, chopped	2 tsp	2 tsp	2 tsp

Slice onion very thin, grate the carrot and chop celery small. If you have a garlic crusher use it to extract the juice, otherwise cook garlic with rest of ingredients and remove before serving. If you have stock from cooking fish use it for this, otherwise use chicken stock cubes. Add prepared vegetables to stock and cook together hard for 5 min, then add vinegar blended with cornflour and stir into vegetables until thickened. Stir in sugar and parsley and serve at once.

Mayonnaise (makes 1¼ cups, ½ pint, 284ml)

Mayonnaise can be made with a hand whisk, an electric beater or an electric blender, but if making by hand beating you need somebody to help you by slowly adding the oil. Personally, I find a blender much quicker and just as effective.

For best results all ingredients should be at room temperature, particularly the oil. If you are unlucky enough to have the mayonnaise curdle—which does happen sometimes—lightly beat an egg yolk in a clean, warm basin and add the mayonnaise to it very gradually, in fact almost drop by drop to begin with, then as it begins to thicken you can add it a little more quickly, blending until smooth.

	USA	Imperial	Metric
egg yolks	2	2	2
salt	½ tsp	½ tsp	½ tsp
dry mustard	½ tsp	½ tsp	½ tsp
castor sugar	½ tsp	½ tsp	½ tsp
lemon juice,			
strained	1 tbsp	1 tbsp	1 tbsp
wine vinegar	1 tbsp	1 tbsp	1 tbsp
olive or salad oil	1¼ cups	½ pint	284ml
boiling water	1 tbsp	1 tbsp	1 tbsp

Many purists say you must use olive oil for mayonnaise, but I find half olive and half corn oil suits us. All vinegar can be used instead of half lemon juice and half vinegar, as you prefer.

Rinse out a bowl in hot water and dry it very well. Put egg yolks into this bowl, add salt, mustard, sugar and half the lemon juice and beat well. Still beating well, have somebody add the oil drop by drop until mayonnaise begins to thicken, then beat in remainder of lemon juice. Continue beating in the oil very slowly until the consistency of thick cream, then add oil in a steady stream, still beating all the time. Beat in vinegar, then slowly add boiling water which prevents separation.

If making in a blender, put egg yolks, vinegar and lemon juice and seasonings into blender. Switch on until well blended then, through the little hole in the lid, gradually pour in the oil, blending all the time. Lastly add boiling water, and blend again.

Mayonnaise variations:

Blue Cheese Dressing: Press 3oz (75g) each of cream cheese and Danish Blue cheese through a sieve and slowly add to above mayonnaise. Beat 8 tbsp (113ml) double cream until thick and fold into mayonnaise.

Tartare Sauce: Add 1 tbsp chopped capers, 1 tbsp chopped gherkins, 1 tbsp chopped parsley and 1 tsp onion juice to above mayonnaise. Serve in halved scooped-out lemons to make cups, sprinkle with paprika, and serve with fish or fish salad.

Cucumber Dressing: Add ½ cup peeled, chopped and drained cucumber,

1 tbsp finely chopped chives and a few grains of cayenne to above mayonnaise, and serve with fish or fish salad.

Thousand Island Dressing: A very popular dressing in the United States to serve over fish salads, hard boiled eggs or green salads. Add 2 finely chopped hard boiled egg yolks, 1 tbsp tomato ketchup, 1 tbsp chili sauce, 2 tsp finely grated onion, and 1 tbsp finely chopped parsley to above mayonnaise.

Anchovy Dressing: Chop 3–4 anchovy fillets very small and add to above mayonnaise with 1 tsp made mustard, 1 tbsp chopped pickled cucumber and 1 tsp grated lemon rind.

Cocktail Sauce: Use this for prawn cocktail or with other seafood. Add 2 tbsp tomato paste, 2 tsp Worcestershire sauce, 2 tsp horseradish sauce, and some paprika to make it a good colour to the above mayonnaise. A little whipped cream can be folded in if desired.

All these are improved by being made some time before serving to allow the flavours to blend.

Yoghurt Dressing

This is good over tossed salads or vegetable salad, or with avocado.

	USA	Imperial	Metric
natural yoghurt	*1 cup*	*8 fl oz*	*226ml*
lemon juice or vinegar	*1 tbsp*	*1 tbsp*	*1 tbsp*
salt and pepper, to taste			
sugar	*2 tsp*	*2 tsp*	*2 tsp*

Beat all these well together, then chill before serving. You can use a mixture of lemon juice and vinegar, or one or the other as preferred.

Soured Cream Dressing

Make as above, but use soured cream instead of the yoghurt.

Piquant Soured Cream Dressing

Make as above then add 1 tsp prepared mustard and 2 tsp Worcestershire sauce.

French Dressing (Sauce Vinaigrette)

There are a number of versions of this simple dressing, depending on individual tastes, but this one is the most usual. I find the easiest way to make it is to put all the ingredients into a jar with a good screw-top and shake well. The garlic can be left in the jar or removed after a few hours just as you like. I always make enough dressing to last a few days, and it keeps quite well—but not in the refrigerator. Shake well before using.

	USA	*Imperial*	*Metric*
olive or salad oil	*4 tbsp*	*4 tbsp*	*4 tbsp*
salt	*½ tsp*	*½ tsp*	*½ tsp*
sugar	*½ tsp*	*½ tsp*	*½ tsp*
dry mustard	*¼ tsp*	*¼ tsp*	*¼ tsp*
garlic, crushed	*1 clove*	*1 clove*	*1 clove*
pepper, freshly ground, to taste			
wine vinegar	*2 tbs*	*2 tbs*	*2 tbs*

Green Dressing (Salsa Verdi)

An Italian dressing using the above dressing as the base. Just add 1 tbsp chopped capers, 1 tbsp very finely chopped chives and 2 tbsp finely chopped parsley. When obtainable fresh, chopped chervil and tarragon can also be added for serving with a tomato salad or with a fish salad.

Part 2. Afters

Cold Puddings & Desserts

All foods need imagination when being prepared but housewives can really let their imagination run riot when preparing and garnishing puddings and desserts, for in this field there are so many ways of adding colour and flavour.

To help make this task easier the supermarket shelves are loaded with all manner of ready-to-serve sweet sauces, canned fruits both familiar and exotic, fruit pie fillings already thickened to the right consistency, pastry cases, sponge flans, meringues, instant custards, cream toppings and an amazing number of different flavoured ice creams.

There are fruit-flavoured yoghurts which can double as sauces, delicious canned Crème de Marrons (chestnut purée), whipped cream from a tube, as well as marvellous frozen cheesecakes or strawberry sponges.

I do not advocate these for everyday desserts, but a good selection of such items in your pantry can save the meal when you suddenly find yourself with 2 or 3 extra people for dinner. Even if your home freezer is well stocked, there are occasions when you haven't even time to thaw out some delectable dessert you made for a special meal.

A few miniature bottles of different liqueurs can also help to make canned fruits or plain ice cream into something special.

Almond and Kirsch Gâteau (serves 6)

Austrian pastrycooks produce the most marvellous cakes and pastries, which are enjoyed at all hours of the day and night accompanied by large cups of coffee topped with a thick layer of whipped cream. These rich cakes are frequently served instead of dessert as the last course for dinner, this one being a good example—and well worth making.

	USA	Imperial	Metric
sponge fingers	18	18	18
milk	¾ cup	6 fl oz	170ml
kirsch	3 tbsp	3 tbsp	3 tbsp
castor sugar	¼ cup	4oz	100g
unsalted butter	¼ cup	4oz	100g
ground almonds	1 cup	4oz	100g
vanilla essence	few drops	few drops	few drops
whipping cream	1¼ cups	½ pint	284ml
flaked, toasted almonds	2 tbsp	2 tbsp	2 tbsp

Using a loaf tin measure a piece of cooking foil or thick greaseproof paper the same width as the tin is long, and cut it so the foil or paper lines the tin with about 2in (5cm) overlapping each side. This is to make it easier to remove the cake from the tin by pulling gently on the overlapping pieces of foil at the same time.

First make the filling. Cream butter and sugar together until light and fluffy. Gradually beat in ground almonds, 2 tbsp kirsch and vanilla essence. Whip half the cream and fold into mixture.

Put milk and remaining kirsch into a shallow soup plate, dip the sponge fingers in this without allowing them to get soggy, and arrange 6 fingers side by side in the lined tin. Spread these with a layer of the almond filling, then cover with another 6 sponge fingers which have been dipped in the milk mixture. Repeat these layers, finishing with a layer of sponge fingers, and put into refrigerator overnight.

Just before serving whip remaining cream and carefully remove gâteau from the tin. Place on a serving plate and swirl the cream over the top, then sprinkle with the almonds. Cut in slices to serve.

Gâteau Viennois (serves 4–6)

This gâteau can be served either as a dessert or a cake, and is a good way of using up the egg yolks after making meringues. It should be made the day before serving, and has the added advantage of needing no cooking.

	USA	Imperial	Metric
butter	4oz	4oz	100g
castor sugar	2 tbsp	2 tbsp	2 tbsp
egg yolks	4	4	4
dark chocolate	4oz	4oz	100g
strong black coffee	1 tbsp	1 tbsp	1 tbsp
stale plain cake or breadcrumbs	10 tbsp	10 tbsp	10 tbsp
cream, whipped, as required			
nuts, chopped, to garnish			

Grate the chocolate and lightly beat egg yolks. Lightly grease a sandwich cake tin with a loose base, or if that is not available use a loaf tin and line it with cooking foil with at least a 2in (5cm) strip of foil overlapping at each side. This makes it easier to remove gâteau from tin.

Cream together butter and sugar, add beaten egg yolks, coffee, grated chocolate and bread or cake crumbs. Mix well together and press into prepared tin. Leave in refrigerator to set. When ready to serve, turn out and cover with whipped cream and chopped nuts.

Chocolate Crumb Cake (serves 6)

A rich dessert which should be made the day before serving.

	USA	Imperial	Metric
cooking chocolate or semi-sweet chocolate pieces	4oz	4oz	100g
rum	2 tbsp	2 tbsp	2 tbsp
instant coffee	2 tsp	2 tsp	2 tsp
egg	1	1	1
double cream, whipped	¼ cup	¼ pint	142ml
walnuts, chopped	½ cup	2½oz	62½g
wholemeal biscuits (Graham crackers)	½lb	½lb	200g
plain chocolate, grated	2 tbsp	2 tbsp	2 tbsp

Break up chocolate and put into heatproof basin with rum. Stand over hot water (not boiling) until melted. Add butter and coffee and mix until smooth. Cool, then add beaten egg and 1 tbsp whipped cream, blending thoroughly, then stir in biscuits which have been crushed to crumbs, and the finely chopped nuts. Line an 8in (20cm) cake tin with foil (use a loose-bottomed one if available) and turn mixture into this, smoothing the top. Chill for 2–3 hr or overnight. Turn out on serving plate, spread top with remainder of whipped cream and sprinkle with grated chocolate.

Crema di Mascherpone (serves 8)

This is a very special recipe from Rome, and it should be served in individual bowls with either fresh strawberries still with their little green caps and stalks intact, or with fingers of fresh pineapple—the idea being that you dunk the pineapple fingers or the strawberries into the delicious cream cheese mixture before eating them. Italian housewives usually make their own cream cheese or ricotta, but you can make it from the ready-prepared kind—so long as it is absolutely fresh.

	USA	Imperial	Metric
cream cheese	1lb	1lb	400g
castor sugar	½ cup	4oz	100g
egg yolks	4	4	4
rum, brandy or kirsch	2 tbsp	2 tbsp	2 tbsp

Put cream cheese through a sieve or blender. Beat egg yolks and sugar together until light and frothy, then add liqueur. Gradually beat this mixture into the cream cheese until it is like thick cream. Chill for 2–3 hr, then divide between individual bowls and serve with strawberries or pineapple fingers.

Crème de Menthe Soufflé (serves 6)
Unlike a baked soufflé, this one can be prepared some time before and brought to the table without any fear that it will collapse if kept waiting.

	USA	Imperial	Metric
eggs, separated	3	3	3
sugar	3 tbsp	3 tbsp	3 tbsp
Crème de Menthe liqueur	2 tbsp	2 tbsp	2 tbsp
gelatine	2 tsp	2 tsp	2 tsp
green colouring	2 drops	2 drops	2 drops
whipping cream	¼ pint	4 fl oz	113ml
dark chocolate	4oz	4oz	100g
nuts, finely chopped	¼ cup	1oz	25g

Using a 2½ cup (1 pint, 568ml) soufflé dish, tie a strip of greaseproof paper round the top to make a collar. Whisk together egg yolks, sugar and liqueur in a basin over a pan of hot water until mixture thickens. Remove from heat, add 1 tbsp cold water and continue beating until mixture cools. Dissolve gelatine in 2 tbsp water, then beat into above mixture. Add just enough green colouring to give a soft tint.

Beat cream and egg whites separately, then add egg whites to cream and beat together until stiff. When gelatine mixture is on point of setting, fold in the cream and egg white mixture. Pour into prepared soufflé dish and chill.

Just before time to serve remove the paper collar and roll edge of soufflé in the chopped nuts. Using a potato peeler, shave off curls from the bar of chocolate and sprinkle over the surface of the soufflé.

If preferred, omit Crème de Menthe and green colouring and substitute brandy or Grand Marnier or any other liqueur. In that case sprinkle top with grated orange rind instead of the chocolate.

Orange and Lemon Cheesecake (serves 6–8)

A well-flavoured cheesecake makes a wonderful finish to a good meal. It has the added advantage that it can be made the day before serving and kept in the refrigerator, then only needs to be garnished immediately before serving. Here are several versions to try.

	USA	Imperial	Metric
eggs	2	2	2
sugar	½ cup	4oz	100g
salt	pinch	pinch	pinch
orange juice	3 tbsp	3 tbsp	3 tbsp
lemon juice	3 tbsp	3 tbsp	3 tbsp
gelatine	½oz	½oz	12½g
cottage cheese	12oz	12oz	300g
double cream	¼ pint	4oz	114ml
digestive biscuits or Graham crackers	½lb	½lb	200g
butter or margarine	4 tbsp	2oz	50g
brown sugar	2 tbsp	2 tbsp	2 tbsp
orange rind, grated, to garnish			

Crush biscuits into crumbs with a rolling pin, then mix well with melted butter or margarine and brown sugar. Press into a deep round cake tin with a loose base and chill while you make the filling.

Beat together egg yolks, half the sugar and salt, then stir in fruit juices. Pour into top of double boiler and cook over boiling water, stirring continuously until mixture thickens and coats the back of the spoon. Soften gelatine in 2 tbsp cold water and stir into mixture, stirring until completely dissolved. Cool. Sieve the cottage cheese and stir into cooled mixture, then fold in whipped cream. Whisk egg whites until stiff, fold in remaining sugar and then fold into mixture. Pour into the cake tin which has been lined with the biscuit mixture and chill until set.

When ready to serve turn out of tin and decorate with grated orange rind sprinkled over the top.

Petit Suisse Flan (serves 4–6)
A different kind of cheesecake which is very simple to make.

	USA	Imperial	Metric
8in (20cm) baked pastry case	1	1	1
cottage cheese	8oz	8oz	200g
yoghurt	5oz	5oz	125g
liquid honey	1 tbsp	1 tbsp	1 tbsp
vanilla essence	¼ tsp	¼ tsp	¼ tsp
strawberries or sliced peaches	½lb	½lb	200g

Sieve the cottage cheese and beat in yoghurt, honey and vanilla essence until well mixed. Spoon mixture into baked pastry case, spreading evenly. Chill for at least 1 hr. Just before serving cut strawberries in halves and arrange cut-side down over the top of the cheese filling, or use canned or fresh peach slices instead.

Chestnut Whip (serves 4–5)
When chestnuts are in season make up this delicious sweet, or to make the job much simpler use canned chestnut purée.

	USA	Imperial	Metric
chestnuts	1lb	1lb	400g
dark chocolate	4oz	4oz	100g
double cream	1¼ cup	½ pint	284ml
icing sugar	2 tbsp	2 tbsp	2 tbsp

Cut a slit in each chestnut, cover with boiling water and boil for 30 min. Drain, peel and remove inner skin, return to clean saucepan, again cover with boiling water and cook until nuts are tender. Press through a sieve or put through a blender until smooth, adding sugar as they blend. Chill until just before serving, then grate the chocolate and mix into chestnut purée, whip the cream until thick and fold in until well blended. Serve at once, or leave in refrigerator until ready to serve.

If preferred, half the grated chocolate can be added to the purée and the remainder used to sprinkle over the top just before serving.

Lemon Mousse (serves 6)

A delicious mousse which can be served just as it is or garnished with fresh strawberries when they are in season.

	USA	*Imperial*	*Metric*
lemon	*1 large*	*1 large*	*1 large*
milk	*1¼ cups*	*½ pint*	*284ml*
cornflour	*2 tsp*	*2 tsp*	*2 tsp*
sugar	*2 tbsp*	*2 tbsp*	*2 tbsp*
eggs	*2*	*2*	*2*
gelatine	*2 tbsp*	*½oz*	*12½g*
cream	*½ cup*	*4oz*	*113ml*

Cut lemon in halves and squeeze out the juice. With a potato peeler carefully cut away yellow part of the lemon rind. Warm the milk and add yellow rind and infuse for about 15 min, then remove rind. Blend cornflour to a smooth paste with a little of the cooled milk, then put milk on to boil and when boiling pour over the blended cornflour, stirring well. Return this mixture to saucepan and stir until boiling and thickened. Add sugar and stir until dissolved. Cool slightly, then beat in the egg yolks. Add lemon juice to gelatine, then add sufficient boiling water to make up to 1¼ cups (½ pint, 284ml), stirring until dissolved. Strain into the cooled custard and whisk well.

Whip the cream until thick and whip egg whites until stiff. Fold half the cream into the egg whites, then fold into custard mixture when it begins to thicken. Pour into fancy mould or basin and chill until set firmly. Turn out and decorate with remainder of whipped cream and strawberries if using.

Pineapple Mouse

Make as above, but instead of dissolving the gelatine in lemon juice and hot water, use pineapple juice drained from a can of pineapple cubes. After turning out the set mould, garnish it with the pineapple cubes.

Mousse au Mocha (serves 8)

This is a very rich dessert so it should only be served in fairly small pots or glasses. If preferred, it can be put into 1 large mould or serving dish.

	USA	Imperial	Metric
semi-sweet chocolate pieces	6oz pkt	6oz pkt	150g pkt
boiling coffee	5 tbsp	5 tbsp	90ml
eggs	4	4	4
dark rum	2 tbsp	2 tbsp	2 tbsp

Dissolve the chocolate in boiling coffee off the heat. Separate yolks and whites of eggs and beat separately. Add beaten egg yolks and rum to chocolate mixture and mix well, then fold in stiffly beaten whites. Divide between 8 small containers and chill.

If making in an electric blender put chocolate pieces and boiling coffee in container and blend until smooth. Add egg yolks and rum and blend until mixed. Beat egg whites until stiff in a bowl, then fold in blended chocolate mixture.

Yorkshire Brandy Snaps (serves 8)

For centuries brandy snaps were sold at country fairs under the name of brandy wafers; they were at first especially popular in Yorkshire, then spread all over England. There were many different kinds of wafers, some of which were made on special irons, and these were taken by housewives when they followed their husbands to the American colonies, and almost certainly were the forerunner of today's popular waffles. Brandy snaps were originally made with brandy as the name implies, but today are made with lemon juice.

They can be made some days before serving and stored in an airtight container, but should not be filled until almost the last minute or they go soft. Rolling them after baking must be done quickly, so don't plan to do anything else until they are all finished.

	USA	Imperial	Metric
golden syrup	*3 tbsp*	*3 tbsp*	*3 tbsp*
butter or margarine	*4 tbsp*	*2oz*	*50g*
castor sugar	*2 tbsp*	*2oz*	*50g*
lemon juice	*1 tsp*	*1 tsp*	*1 tsp*
plain flour	*½ cup*	*2oz*	*50g*
ground ginger	*1 tsp*	*1 tsp*	*1 tsp*
whipped cream, as required			

Place golden syrup, margarine or butter, sugar and lemon juice in a small saucepan, heat slowly until melted, then remove from heat. Sift flour and ground ginger together and stir into syrup mixture. Cool. Lightly grease 3 baking sheets, and using a teaspoon, drop 4 or 5 spoonfuls of mixture on each baking sheet, keeping them well apart to allow for spreading. Bake for about 8 min in a moderate oven (350° F, 180° C, Gas Mark 4) or until deep golden brown, baking only one lot at a time. Remove from oven and place second lot into bake. Carefully loosen brandy snaps with a spatula, and using the handle of a wooden spoon roll brandy snap round the handle, pressing gently to join the overlapping sides and hold until set. Remove spoon handle and place rolled brandy snap on wire rack to cool. Quickly roll remainder, but if they should set on baking sheet and are difficult to remove, put back into oven for about 2 min. Repeat this procedure with all the snaps as they are baked. Be sure they are quite cold before storing, or if serving at once fill each one with whipped cream, using an icing bag to force cream into rolled snap.

These amounts should make about 16–18 snaps, and I usually find that 2 each is quite adequate as a dessert after a main meal. The whipped cream can be flavoured with a little brandy if desired.

Brandy Snap Cream Cake (serves 8)

A variation of the above recipe is to make up the mixture with the addition of chopped nuts, then bake in 3 or 4 layers. This is best done by placing an 8in (20cm) flan ring on a greased oven tray then spooning enough of the mixture into the ring to make a thin layer. Bake as above, repeating this for each layer. Remove ring and lift brandy snap

Page 135   (*above*) Strawberry and cottage cheese ring; (*below*) meringue topping

Page 136 (*right*) Marinara flan; (*below*) St Nicholas wreath

very carefully with a wide spatula or egg slice on to a wire rack to cool
—do not roll but leave quite flat.

When quite cold, sandwich the layers together with either whipped
cream or ice cream and put into freezer for 1 hr before serving.

Fruit Salads

Fruit salad made from a combination of fresh fruits is a dessert which
is always appreciated because rarely do you use the same fruits, as each
time you make it there are different fruits available.

A fruit salad can be a simple combination of 2 or 3 fruits, such as orange
slices, diced bananas and canned pineapple, or it can be a glorious mixture of all the summer fruits which come into season at the same time.

But a fruit salad can also be interesting in winter, following a hearty
casserole or stew, and for this you can combine cooked prunes and
cooked dried apricots, oranges, grapefruit and chopped preserved
ginger, adding a very little of the ginger syrup for extra flavour.

Always prepare a fruit salad a few hours before serving to allow the
sugar to dissolve and form a syrup with the fruit juices. For special
occasions a little brandy, rum or kirsch, or one of the fruit liqueurs can
be added.

And serve it chilled—but not frozen. Certainly, fruit salads will freeze
well, but allow them to thaw before serving to get the best flavour.

THE STRAWBERRY SEASON

Strawberries have only a short season, so make the most of them when
they are available. Certainly, there are canned and frozen strawberries
all the year round, and they can be used for most of these following
recipes when the fresh varieties are finished, but let us use these delicate
globes of sweetness while at their best.

There are many different kinds of strawberries, and many ways of
using them, but nothing can really improve on the traditional dish of a
rosy mound of berries on a plate, lightly sprinkled with castor sugar,
with thick cream to pour over the top.

I always remember my first wood strawberries in Italy, and how disappointed I was when they arrived at the table, they were so tiny and insignificant-looking. But what a delicious aroma they had, and the taste—it was wonderful, quite unlike any other berries I had ever had.

Try to avoid buying any berries after heavy rain, for the wet causes them to deteriorate very quickly. When buying in a punnet or box check that the base of the box is not stained with juice. If it is, the chances are that the bottom layers of the fruit are damaged and probably squashed.

Strawberry Whip (serves 6)

	USA	Imperial	Metric
strawberries	1 lb	1 lb	400g
sweet sherry or orange juice	2 tsp	2 tsp	2 tsp
egg whites	2	2	2
castor sugar	2 tbsp	2 tbsp	2 tbsp
whipping cream	1¼ cups	½ pint	284ml

Wash and hull strawberries and put aside 6 of the best-looking berries to use as a garnish. Chop remainder of berries and put into a bowl with sherry or orange juice and 2 tsp sugar. Mix lightly and put into a cool place for at least 1 hr.

Just before serving time whip egg whites until stiff, then gradually beat in sugar until meringue is stiff and glossy. Whip the cream until thick and fold into meringue, then lastly fold in strawberries. Divide between 6 sweet dishes and top each with a whole strawberry.

Raspberries or loganberries can be prepared in the same way.

Strawberry Brulée (serves 6)

A marvellous dessert if you have somebody in the kitchen to prepare this at the last minute before serving.

	USA	Imperial	Metric
strawberries	1 lb	1 lb	40g
raspberries	½ lb	½ lb	200g
icing sugar	2½ tbsp	1 oz	25g
whipping cream	¼ pint	4 fl oz	113ml
soft brown sugar	¼ cup	2 oz	50g

Wash and hull the strawberries and place in a shallow ovenproof dish, chill for at least 1 hr. Wash raspberries and put through a sieve. Sift icing sugar over the raspberry purée and stir well, then pour over strawberries. Beat cream until fairly stiff and spread evenly over the fruit. Chill until just before serving.

Pre-heat the grill. Sprinkle top of cream evenly with the brown sugar (there should be a good layer), and put under grill until sugar is caramelised, but be careful it does not brown too much. Serve at once.

Strawberries Marie-Thérèse (serves 8)

	USA	Imperial	Metric
strawberries	1 lb	1 lb	400g
redcurrants	1 lb	1 lb	400g
raspberries	1 lb	1 lb	400g
lemon juice	2 tsp	2 tsp	2 tsp
orange juice	1 tbsp	1 tbsp	1 tbsp
sugar, to taste			
whipping cream	¼ pint	4 fl oz	113ml

All the fruit should be absolutely fresh and well ripened. Wash and hull fruit, draining them very well, then mix all together in a serving bowl. Add fruit juices and sugar to taste and chill for at least 1 hr. Remove from refrigerator 10 min before serving and top with lightly sweetened whipped cream.

Instead of the fruit juices add some sweet white wine such as Sauterne.

Strawberries Martinique

Wash and hull required number of firm, ripe strawberries, sprinkle with rum and chill. 10 min before serving top with soured cream sweetened to taste with Demerara sugar.

Strawberries Seville (serves 10–12)

This is an attractive dessert to serve for a summer buffet party when strawberries are plentiful. It looks its best when made in a big glass bowl, and just slightly chilled.

	USA	Imperial	Metric
strawberries	4lb	4lb	1kg 600g
oranges	4 large	4 large	4 large
egg whites	2	2	2
whipping cream	1¼ cups	½ pint	284ml
castor sugar	2 tbsp	2 tbsp	2 tbsp

Wash and hull strawberries, drain well and after reserving 6 of the best berries for a garnish, cut remainder in halves and place in large glass bowl.

Peel oranges and cut out each segment quite free of white pith and membranes. Add to strawberries and mix lightly, adding 1 tbsp sugar. chill.

Whip egg whites until stiff, then fold in remaining tbsp sugar. Whip cream until thick and fold in egg whites. (A few drops vanilla essence may be added if desired.) Chill. Just before serving cover fruit with a layer of cream, roughing it up unevenly all over. Garnish with extra berries.

Strawberry and Cottage Cheese Ring (serves 6–8)
A delicious way of using up the smaller late strawberries, or frozen ones at other times of the year. The combination of berries and cottage cheese is very good to finish a dinner party.

	USA	Imperial	Metric
strawberries	½lb	½lb	200g
strawberry jelly	1 Jello	1 pkt	1 pkt
cottage cheese	1lb	1lb	400g
honey	1 tbsp	1 tbsp	1 tbsp
double cream	¼ pint	4 fl oz	113ml
gelatine	2 tsp	2 tsp	2 tsp
water	1 tbsp	1 tbsp	1 tbsp
lemon juice	2 tsp	2 tsp	2 tsp
boiling water	1¾ cups	¾ pint	424ml

Dissolve jelly in boiling water and leave to cool. Dampen a 6½in (16·5cm) ring mould and pour 3 tbsp jelly into the bottom. Arrange a pattern of strawberry halves in this and leave to set. Sieve cottage cheese and combine with honey, whip cream until thick and fold into mixture. Dissolve gelatine in 1 tbsp water and lemon juice over a pan of hot water, fold into cottage cheese mixture and spoon into mould when first layer is set firmly. Chill until this layer is set, then pour in remaining jelly and arrange remainder of strawberries. Chill well to set. Turn out carefully and serve.

Strawberry Syllabub (serves 6)

Recipes for syllabubs have been found in many ancient cookery books, and they are a feature of medieval dinners as presented today in many British castles and stately homes for tourists. There are a number of different ways of making these syllabubs and these two versions are worth trying at home.

	USA	Imperial	Metric
strawberries	½lb	½lb	200g
orange	1 large	1 large	1 large
Grand Marnier liqueur	1 tbsp	1 tbsp	1 tbsp
castor sugar	3 tbsp	3 tbsp	3 tbsp
white wine	½ pint	4 fl oz	113ml
lemon juice	1 tsp	1 tsp	1 tsp
whipping cream	1¼ cups	½ pint	284ml
egg whites	2	2	2

Wash and hull berries, slice and arrange in 6 dessert glasses. Grate rind from orange, then squeeze the juice. Add juice and liqueur to strawberries. Put sugar, wine, lemon juice and half grated orange rind in bowl, add cream and stir well. Whisk egg whites until stiff, add to cream mixture and continue whisking until mixture is thick. Spoon on top of strawberries, sprinkle tops with remainder of orange rind. Chill well before serving.

Raspberry Syllabub (serves 4–5)

	USA	Imperial	Metric
raspberries	½ lb	½ lb	200g
lemon	1 small	1 small	1 small
white wine	4 tbsp	4 tbsp	4 tbsp
sherry	2 tbsp	2 tbsp	2 tbsp
whipping cream	1¼ cups	½ pint	284ml
castor sugar	2 tbsp	2 tbsp	2 tbsp

Wash and drain raspberries well, using only good quality, ripe berries. Peel rind from half the lemon, removing all the soft white pith. Put into a bowl with the wine, sherry and strained juice from the lemon and leave for 2 hr, stirring several times. Whisk the cream (use a hand whisk) until just thickening, strain the wine mixture into cream and add half the raspberries, mixing lightly together. Pour into a large glass dish, decorate with remainder of berries and serve.

Pineapple Royale (serves 6)

This is a dessert to make for a special dinner when you can obtain a large ripe pineapple with a good crown of leaves.

	USA	Imperial	Metric
pineapple	1 large	1 large	1 large
strawberries	1 lb	1 lb	400g
rum or orange juice	2 tbsp	2 tbsp	2 tbsp
sugar	1 tbsp	1 tbsp	1 tbsp
whipping cream	1¼ cups	½ pint	284ml

Cut pineapple in halves lengthwise right through the crown of leaves, which should be wiped over with a damp cloth. Carefully cut out pineapple pulp, leaving a smooth shell, and be careful not to pierce this skin. Chill until ready to serve.

Cut away core of pineapple and dice remainder of flesh, being sure to remove the eyes. Wash and hull the strawberries and put into a bowl with the pineapple cubes, rum or orange juice and half the sugar.

Chill for some hours. Whip the cream, adding remainder of sugar.

When ready to serve arrange pineapple halves on a large serving plate with the leaves at alternate ends. Fill with the fruit (draining away most of the juice, which can be used for another dessert next day). Put half the whipped cream into an icing bag and pipe round the edge of each pineapple shell to make a border. Put remainder of cream into a bowl and serve separately.

When strawberries are not available use either melon balls or diced fresh peaches.

Pineapple Lisa (serves 6)

This is another version of the above dish, using raspberries instead of strawberries, and Grand Marnier is used instead of rum. After pineapple cubes and raspberries are replaced in the pineapple shells they are covered with meringue (p 176) and put into a fairly hot oven (400° F, 200° C, Gas Mark 7) just long enough to tint the meringue golden, then served at once, with either whipped cream or ice cream.

A MEDLEY OF MELON RECIPES

Just as melons come in many different kinds, so can they be used in many different ways, either as the beginning of a meal (see p 143) or to finish it.

They can be cut in halves, the seeds scooped out and the hollows filled with ice cream—which seems to be the most popular way, or do as is done in the north of Portugal, in the port wine country. Here a favourite way of serving them is to scoop out the seeds from the ripe ½ melons, prick the flesh all over with a fork, then pour some port into the hollow of the fruit, leaving it to stand in a cool place until ready to serve. Or you can scoop out the melon pulp with a ball-cutter, mix with equal quantities of cubed fresh pineapple, add the port wine and replace in the melon shells.

Melon and Grapefruit Delight (serves 4)

grapefruit	*2 large*
melon	*1 medium*

sherry or rum	*to taste*	
sugar	*to taste*	
bottled cherries	*4*	

Roll the grapefruit lightly on a table to release the juices, then cut each in halves 'through the equator'. With a curved grapefruit knife cut out the centre pith, then remove the pulp. Remove the membranes separating the segments, and cut away any white pith on the grapefruit pieces. Replace the segments in the shells as tidily as possible.

Peel the melon and remove seeds, then cut into wedges. Insert a wedge of melon between each grapefruit segment. Add sherry or rum and sweeten to taste. Place each prepared half in an individual sweet dish and chill for at least 1 hr before serving. Drain and dry cherries and place each one in centre of each ½ grapefruit.

Cantaloupe à la Mode (serves 6)

	USA	Imperial	Metric
cantaloupe	*1 large*	*1 large*	*1 large*
vanilla ice cream	*4 cups*	*1¼ pints*	*850ml*
orange rind, grated	*2 tbsp*	*2 tbsp*	*2 tbsp*

Slice cantaloupe into 6 rings, peel and remove seeds. Place each slice on a chilled plate, fill centre with a scoop of ice cream and sprinkle with grated orange rind. Serve at once.

Jellied Melon Surprise (serves 4)
Make this the day before it is to be served.

	USA	Imperial	Metric
ripe melon	*1 large*	*1 large*	*1 large*
lemon-flavoured jelly	*1 Jello*	*1 pkt*	*1 pkt (135g)*
orange juice	*½ cup*	*4 fl oz*	*113ml*
sweet sherry or rum	*1 tbsp*	*1 tbsp*	*1 tbsp*

The melon should be of a good size, ripe without being too soft.

Wash it well, cut in halves lengthwise and scoop out the seeds. Make it sit firmly by cutting a small slice from the underside of each half. Add the sherry or rum to each half and leave to stand while you make the filling.

Dissolve jelly in half quantity of boiling water called for in directions on packet, add orange juice and enough cold water, less 1 tbsp, to make up required amount. Chill until just thickening, then beat well, adding sherry or rum and juices which have collected in the melon halves. An electric blender does this job quickly and easily.

Divide the jelly between the two halves of the melon. Any jelly remaining can be set in a small bowl, then chopped and added to melons when set. Chill until firmly set, then cut each half into 2 to give 4 quarters. Serve as it is or with ice cream.

Watermelon Delight (serves 8–12)

Delicious for a dinner party when watermelons are in season, this looks most attractive as it is served in the watermelon shell.

Cut a medium-sized ripe watermelon in halves, then scoop out the pink flesh, using a ball-cutter or a round teaspoon. Be careful to remove all the seeds. Cover the melon shells with foil or put into a polythene bag and store in refrigerator until time for serving. The edge of the melon can be scalloped if liked.

Put melon balls into a large bowl with a mixture of strawberries, diced pineapple, diced fresh peaches, and diced peeled apples, or any other fruits available. Pour 8 tbsp (113ml) of rum, Madeira or port wine, or a miniature bottle of Kirsch over the fruit and chill until ready to serve. If preferred, orange juice can be added instead of the alcohol. Mix all together lightly.

Turn the fruit into the melon shells and bring to the table to serve with whipped cream or ice cream, or it is quite good without any other dressing.

Caramel Oranges (serves 6)

These are a speciality of several of the best-known restaurants in Rome, where they are an expensive delicacy. You can serve them to your guests at the price of a little effort during the afternoon of your dinner party.

	USA	Imperial	Metric
oranges	6	6	6
sugar	½lb	½lb	200g
kirsch or Orange	1 tbsp	1 tbsp	1 tbsp
Curaçao liqueur			
water	1¼ cups	½ pint	284ml

Use navel oranges when available, and choose them all as nearly the same size as possible. Using a potato peeler cut the orange peel from 2 oranges as thinly as possible. Cut this peel into strips as fine as matches, put into boiling water and cook at boiling point for about 7 min, then drain and dry well.

Carefully peel all the oranges so they are free of any white pith, and remove cores as neatly as possible. Make a syrup by cooking sugar and water together until thick and like a caramel, then dip oranges into syrup, turning to coat evenly with the caramel. Place the coated oranges on a shallow serving dish in one layer. Put prepared peel into syrup and cook until nearly transparent. Place a spoonful of this peel on top of each orange, and chill until serving time.

Oranges San Francisco (serves 4)

This is a simple dessert which I enjoyed very much in that lovely city of San Francisco, but there are doubtless many other cities which make a claim to the same recipe.

	USA	Imperial	Metric
large navel oranges	4	4	4
fresh orange juice	½ cup	4 fl oz	113ml
whipping cream	1 cup	8 fl oz	226ml
sugar, to taste			
Orange Curaçao liqueur,			
to taste			

Grate the rind of 1 orange and add to orange juice. Peel all the oranges carefully, removing all the white pith, then cut in even slices. Place the slices in overlapping rows in a shallow rectangular dish. If using the liqueur add it to orange juice, when it should be sweet enough, but otherwise add a little sugar to taste and stir until dissolved. Pour this gently over the orange slices and chill for at least 1 hr. Whip the cream, adding sugar to taste, and just before serving spoon it over the oranges.

If preferred, ice cream can be used instead of whipped cream.

Peaches Tropicale (serves 6)

A simple and delicious dessert for a hot night.

	USA	Imperial	Metric
fresh peaches	6	6	6
fresh orange juice	¾ cup	¼ pint	170ml
lemon juice	2 tsp	2 tsp	2 tsp
clear honey	2 tbsp	2 tbsp	2 tbsp
brandy or sweet sherry if desired	2–3 tsp	2–3 tsp	2–3 tsp

Prepare these several hours before serving to blend the flavours and chill well.

Peel and slice peaches into a serving bowl. Mix together orange and lemon juices with the honey and brandy or sherry if using and pour over peaches. Leave in a cool place to chill until just before serving. Can be served alone or with whipped cream or ice cream.

Figs Tropicale

Fresh ripe figs are superb when peeled and sliced and prepared as in the above recipe. I use rum instead of brandy for these.

5-Cup Sweet Salad (serves 6)

	USA	Imperial	Metric
drained canned grapefruit	1 cup	8 fl oz	226ml
coconut	1 cup	2½oz	60g
marshmallows, chopped	1 cup	2oz	50g
canned crushed pineapple	1 cup	8 fl oz	226ml
sour cream	1 cup	8 fl oz	226ml
bottled cherries	6	6	6

147

Drain the fruit well before measuring. It may be simpler for British housewives to use a cup for measuring every ingredient, but the same cup must be used for all measurements.

Mix coconut, marshmallows and sour cream together, then fold in drained fruit and chill. Serve in 6 glass bowls and garnish each with a cherry.

If preferred, crushed wholemeal biscuits (Graham crackers) may be used instead of coconut.

Caribbean Cream (serves 4–5)

	USA	Imperial	Metric
bananas	2	2	2
light brown sugar	2 tbsp	2 tbsp	2 tbsp
sour cream	1 cup	8 fl oz	226ml
canned crushed pineapple	1¼ cups	1 cup	284ml
dark chocolate	2oz	2oz	50g

Drain pineapple. Using an electric blender put in peeled bananas, sugar, sour cream and 2 tbsp pineapple juice and blend for 20 sec. Mix into crushed pineapple, blending well, then divide between 4 or 5 individual dishes. Using a potato peeler, make curls of chocolate to use as a garnish, or grate on a coarse grater.

By thinning this down with a little more pineapple juice this makes a delicious sauce to pour over ice cream.

Quick Trifle (serves 6)

	USA	Imperial	Metric
Swiss roll or sponge cake	6 slices	6 slices	6 slices
canned mandarin oranges	11oz can	11oz can	275g can
sweet sherry or port	4 tbsp	4 tbsp	4 tbsp
bananas	3	3	3
canned custard	15oz can	15oz can	375g can
whipping cream	¼ pint	4 fl oz	113ml
chopped nuts	4 tbsp	4 tbsp	4 tbsp

Cut Swiss roll or sponge cake into 6 slices. Using 6 tall dessert glasses put a spoonful of custard into each glass, then add a slice of cake. Add 2 tbsp mandarin juice to the sherry or port and sprinkle some of this over cake. Add drained mandarin oranges, sliced bananas, and custard in that order, sprinkling with the sherry and juice. Cover with whipped cream and sprinkle top with nuts. Chill well if you have time.

If mandarin oranges are not available use well-drained canned peach slices.

Apple Yoghurt Whip (serves 4)

This is a good dessert for slimmers if the apple is sweetened with one of the liquid sweeteners instead of sugar.

	USA	Imperial	Metric
stewed apples	2½ cups	1 pint	568ml
lemon juice	1 tbsp	1 tbsp	1 tbsp
plain yoghurt	¼ pint	4 fl oz	113ml
sweetening, to taste			

Beat apples until the consistency of a smooth sauce, then beat in yoghurt and lemon juice. Sweeten to taste. Chill well before serving.

Orange juice and 2 tsp grated orange rind can be substituted for the lemon juice for a change.

Apple and Ginger Layers

Using individual glass goblets put in alternate layers of stewed apples, crushed gingernut biscuits and either sour cream or plain yoghurt. Chill well before serving.

Desserts with Meringue

Whites of eggs beaten up with sugar to make a meringue can add a special finish to the simplest of desserts. They have the added advantage that you can make up meringue cases and separate toppings, bake them until crisp, then keep them for days if stored in an air-tight container ready for when you want to use them.

If you have an electric beater you will find meringues much easier to make, but a good rotary beater will also do a good job—it only needs more effort on the part of the cook.

Take eggs out of the refrigerator some time before using for meringues—at room temperature they will beat up more easily. Always use a perfectly dry basin and a dry beater, and be very careful that not even a speck of yolk goes into the white when breaking, or they will not beat up stiffly enough. When beating the egg whites they should be stiff enough to hold their shape well, but also look moist and glossy, not dry. When folding the last part of the sugar into egg whites use a metal fork or spoon—not a wooden one.

The basic meringue mixture given here can be used to make a meringue shell; meringue discs to use as a topping or to build up into a delicious torte; to make small meringues to use as a garnish on ice cream or fruit, and the Pavlova cake which has become almost the national dish of Australia. And you can also make that very special dessert, a Baked Alaska.

There are several schools of thought about the type of sugar to be used for meringues—some cooks use only castor sugar, others prefer granulated sugar, while others use half castor and half granulated. I prefer the latter, but I have made excellent meringues using all granulated sugar, in which case care must be taken to be sure it is completely dissolved in the egg whites. I also add a little white vinegar or lemon juice and ½ tsp cornflour to the mixture.

Basic Meringue Mixture

	USA	Imperial	Metric
egg whites	4	4	4
castor sugar	½ cup	4oz	100g
granulated sugar	½ cup	4oz	100g
salt, pinch			
white vinegar	1 tsp	1 tsp	1 tsp
cornflour	½ tsp	½ tsp	½ tsp

For the meringue shell or Pavlova draw an 8in (20cm) circle on a piece of thick white paper and brush over well with vegetable oil. Place paper on an oven tray.

For the torte and the toppings you will need 2 circles.

Make meringue by beating egg whites and salt until stiff. Gradually beat in half the sugar, a spoonful at a time, then fold in remainder of sugar, with vinegar and cornflour, keeping it very light but well mixed.

Bake in a slow oven (250° F, 130° C, Gas Mark ½) for about 1½ hr or until meringue is set. Be careful it does not colour too much, it should be just creamy-coloured. Remove from oven and allow to cool slightly on a rack, then peel away the paper, handling the meringues with care as they are very brittle. Be sure they are completely cold before storing if not being used at once.

For the meringue shell spread the basic mixture over the oiled paper in an 8in (20cm) circle, building up the sides about 2in (5cm) high, and leaving a base at least ¾in (2cm) thick. Bake as directed above.

For the torte or to use as a topping, divide the basic mixture between 2 prepared circles, smooth over the tops to make them even, and bake as above.

Meringue Toppings

A simple fruit pie or plain stewed fruit can be made into something rather special if topped with a meringue baked separately, then assembled just before serving.

These toppings can be made at the same time as you are making a Pavlova, then after baking they will keep for at least a week if stored in an air-tight container.

A special way of making these is to use an icing pipe. First mark a circle of the desired size—one that will fit over an 8in (20cm) pie dish is good—then using thick greaseproof paper or parchment, fill the icing bag with the meringue mixture and pipe it in circles, starting from the middle and extending outwards, something like the shell of a snail. Stud at intervals with blanched almonds and bake as directed on page 151.

PAVLOVA

The first Pavlova was made by an Australian hostess in honour of the great ballerina who was at that time visiting Australia—or so the story goes, and I know of no other explanation for this delicious meringue dessert. To be a *real* Pavlova it must have a filling of passion fruit folded into stiffly whipped cream, but as this delectable fruit is not easily obtainable, other fruits, such as strawberries, raspberries and peaches, can be substituted.

The meringue shell can also be filled with creamy mixtures flavoured with lemon or chocolate such as given here, which can be made with the egg yolks left after making the meringue.

Lemon Pavlova (serves 6–8)

	USA	Imperial	Metric
egg yolks	4	4	4
lemon juice	3 tbsp	3 tbsp	3 tbsp
lemon rind, grated	1 tbsp	1 tbsp	1 tbsp
castor sugar	¼ cup	2oz	50g
double cream	½ cup	4oz	100g
bottled cherries, for garnishing			

Beat egg yolks until well mixed, then very slowly beat in the castor sugar. Lastly add strained lemon juice and the grated rind and mix well.

Using a double saucepan, place the lemon mixture in the top section, with gently bubbling water in lower half, but the water in lower container should not touch the base of the top part, for the mixture *must not* boil. Stir mixture continuously until thickened and smooth, you can tell when it is cooked as it will almost 'sheet' from the spoon. Allow to get quite cold.

Just before serving spread lemon mixture into the meringue case, then cover with stiffly whipped cream and garnish with chopped cherries.

Pineapple Pavlova (serves 6–8)

Substitute canned pineapple juice for the lemon juice in above recipe, and use only 1 tsp grated lemon rind. After filling meringue case with this pineapple mixture, cover it with a layer of well-drained crushed or chopped pineapple, then cover with the whipped cream.

Chocolate Pavlova (serves 6–8)

Make a meringue case as in above recipe (*p* 151) and fill it with this rich and delicious chocolate mixture for a very special occasion. When you are feeling really extravagant, substitute rum for the water when melting the chocolate, or use half water and half rum. Make some hours before serving.

K

...

	USA	Imperial	Metric
semi-sweet chocolate pieces	6oz pkt	6oz pkt	150g pkt
egg yolks	4	4	4
water or rum	½ cup	4oz	113ml
double cream	1¼ cups	½ pint	284ml
sugar	¼ cup	2oz	50g

Melt the chocolate pieces over hot water. Cool slightly, then spread 3 tbsp of this over the base of the cooked and cooled meringue case. Allow to set hard.

To the remaining melted chocolate add the egg yolks and water, mixing well. Cook in the top of a double saucepan (see above) until mixture thickens. Chill. Whip cream with the sugar until thick, and spread half over the hardened chocolate in the meringue. Fold remainder into the chocolate mixture and spread it on top. Chill several hours before serving. May be garnished with chopped nuts if liked.

Meringue Torten (serves 6–8)

Different flavoured torten or meringue cakes can be made using the basic meringue recipe (p 151), divided into two and used to cover two 8in (20cm) circles of oiled paper, spreading to an even depth all over, then baking as directed. These can be made up some days before serving and kept in an air-tight container, but be sure they are completely cold before storing or filling.

Lemon Torte: Use same filling as for Lemon Pavlova (p 153) to sandwich the two meringue circles together, spreading also over the top circle, then cover completely with whipped cream and decorate with chopped cherries.

Pineapple Torte: Use same filling as for Pineapple Pavlova (p 153) and follow above directions, but decorate with pieces of pineapple.

Chocolate Nut Torte: Add chopped nuts and grated dark chocolate to stiffly whipped cream, sandwich circles together and cover top with the flavoured cream. Decorate with more grated chocolate.

Strawberry Torte: Add quartered strawberries to stiffly whipped cream for filling and topping. Garnish with whole berries.

After filling, chill all the above for some hours before serving.

Mocha Meringues (serves 6)

This recipe can be used to make small meringues which can be sand-
wiched together in pairs with whipped cream or ice cream, or you can
make small meringue cases which can be filled with ice cream.

	USA	Imperial	Metric
egg whites	2	2	2
castor sugar	4 tbsp	4 tbsp	4 tbsp
cocoa	2 tsp	2 tsp	2 tsp
instant coffee	1 tsp	1 tsp	1 tsp
salt	pinch	pinch	pinch

Beat egg whites until stiff and dry, then beat in half the sugar which
has been sifted with cocoa, coffee and salt. Fold in remainder of sugar
mixture until well blended. Put meringues on to a greased baking tray
in whatever shape is needed, shaping them with a metal spoon. Bake
in a cool oven (275° F, 140° C, Gas Mark 1) for 1½ hr or until crisp.

When cool, sandwich together with whipped cream or ice cream.
Add roughly chopped walnuts and some grated chocolate to the
whipped cream for a special filling if you have made individual
meringue cases.

Apple Meringues

Make individual meringue cases as directed above, and fill them with
slightly tart apple purée, then cover with whipped cream to which a
little sugar and a pinch of cinnamon has been added.

Raspberry Vacherin (serves 6)

This is a recipe I first tasted at the wine festival luncheon at Neuchâtel,
in Switzerland; a delicious sweet for a very happy occasion, as the
wines from this area are well worth trying. The vacherin is an ideal
recipe for those with a home freezer, as it can be made up when raspberries are plentiful, frozen and then served at any time you need a
really special dessert.

	USA	Imperial	Metric
egg whites	4	4	4
castor sugar	14 tbsp	7oz	175g
plain flour	12 tbsp	3oz	75g
butter, melted	4 tbsp	2oz	50g
ground almonds	7 tbsp	3oz	75g
salt	pinch	pinch	pinch
raspberries	1lb	1lb	400g
whipping cream	1¼ cups	½ pint	284ml
icing sugar	2 tsp	2 tsp	2 tsp

Whip egg whites with salt until stiff, fold in sugar sifted with flour, ground almonds and cooled melted butter, keeping the mixture as light as possible.

Have 3 8in (20cm) circles drawn on oiled paper and spread meringue mixture on these, keeping them as evenly spread as possible. Bake in a fairly slow oven (300° F, 150° C, Gas Mark 2) until crisp and pale golden. Very carefully remove paper and cool on wire racks. If preferred the meringue mixture can be baked in 3 8in (20cm) sandwich tins with loose bases.

Whip cream until stiff, sweeten to taste and add the raspberries. Sandwich the meringue layers together with the raspberry cream, and chill for at least 30 min if serving on the day it is made.

To freeze, stand finished vacherin on a foil plate and freeze unwrapped. When frozen hard, wrap carefully in foil or polythene, or put into a plastic box, and label. When ready to serve do not thaw completely, as it is easier to cut if still firm.

Strawberries or redcurrants can be used in place of raspberries if preferred.

Ice Cream Desserts

With a few trays of home-made ice cream or some commercially packaged ice cream in several flavours in the freezing section of your refrigerator or in the home freezer it is possible to make a great variety of different desserts both for family meals and for special dinner parties with very little trouble.

If the freezer section of your refrigerator is large enough, iced bombes can be made up days beforehand and kept frozen until they are wanted for a party, using either home-made or commercial ice cream, and adding various flavours of your own choice.

Plain fruit sorbets, once served to clear the palate between rich courses of Victorian dinner parties, are becoming increasingly popular as desserts, not only because they are less fattening but also because of their delicious flavours.

Remember to set your refrigerator control at its coldest temperature before commencing to make the ice cream to enable it to freeze as quickly as possible. Home freezers do not need to be adjusted when making ice cream. Have all utensils well chilled before starting.

Care should be taken not to beat cream too stiff for ice cream as this makes the mixture too heavy. Too much sugar is also a bad fault, as it slows down freezing.

Always remember to take the ice cream from the refrigerator or freezer some time before serving to allow it to come to the right consistency. And don't forget to adjust the temperature control when you have removed ice cream from the freezing compartment of your refrigerator.

Rich Ice Cream (serves 4–5)

	USA	Imperial	Metric
egg whites	2	2	2
double cream	5 fl oz	¼ pint	142ml
single cream	5 fl oz	¼ pint	142ml
icing sugar	2 tbsp	2oz	50g
vanilla essence	½ tsp	½ tsp	½ tsp

Beat double cream until just thickening, then beat in single cream. Add sugar and flavouring. Beat egg whites until stiff, fold in cream, blending together lightly, and pour into freezing tray. Freeze until firm. This mixture does not need to be beaten again.

Economy Ice Cream (serves 6)

	USA	Imperial	Metric
milk	2½ cups	1 pint	568ml
sugar	1 rounded tbsp	2 dessert sp	2 dessert sp
gelatine	½ tsp	½ tsp	½ tsp
water	1 tbsp	1 tbsp	1 tbsp
vanilla essence	½ tsp	½ tsp	½ tsp
powdered milk	4 tbsp	2oz	50g

Beat powdered milk into the fresh milk, add gelatine which has been dissolved in warm water, sugar and flavouring, and beat until mixture is smooth and creamy. Pour into freezing tray and freeze until there is a ½in (generous 1cm) frozen border all round tray. Turn mixture into a chilled basin and beat until nearly doubled in bulk. Pour back into freezing tray and freeze until set. Turn temperature control halfway back to normal until ready to serve.

Flavour Variations

Italian: When making Rich Ice Cream beat 2 egg yolks until creamy and add to whipped cream before folding in the beaten egg whites. Add a few drops each of vanilla, almond and lemon essences.

Berry: Add crushed berries and a few drops of red food colouring to ice cream before freezing.

Chocolate: Melt 2oz (2 squares) chocolate over hot water. Cool and add to basic recipe.

Chocolate Chip: As above, only grate chocolate instead of melting it, then fold into mixture.

Chocolate Mint: Melt 4oz (100g) chocolate mint creams in a basin over hot water. Stir into half-frozen ice cream after second beating. It should be swirled through the mixture, not beaten in.

Coffee and Cognac: Blend 1 tbsp instant coffee and 2 tsp castor sugar with 2 tbsp brandy and beat into mixture before freezing.

Ginger: Omit vanilla, add 2 tbsp chopped preserved ginger and 2 tsp ginger syrup.

Mocha Walnut: Add 2 tsp instant coffee powder, 2 tsp cocoa and 1 tbsp chopped walnuts to mixture before freezing.

Sauced Ice Cream

A quick and easy sweet is made by serving 1 or 2 scoops or slices of ice cream for each person in well-chilled bowls, and with them serve 3 or 4 different sauces (*p* 204) for guests to help themselves.

Chocolate Meringue Sundaes

Make chocolate meringues as directed on page 155. Put alternate layers of vanilla ice cream (*p* 158) and roughly crushed meringues in tall glasses, finishing with a layer of ice cream and sprinkle tops with grated chocolate or chopped nuts.

Or use chocolate ice cream (*p* 159) and plain meringues, crumbled, and top with whipped cream sprinkled with grated chocolate.

Mandarino Sundae

Put alternate layers of vanilla ice cream and drained canned mandarin oranges in tall glasses. For a special sweet, add a little Orange Curaçao liqueur to the mandarin juice and pour over the top of each sundae.

Avocado and Pineapple Delight (serves 6)

This is a recipe from Brazil, and if you have never tasted avocado as a sweet course instead of a beginning you will be pleasantly surprised by this one. The avocado should be just slightly soft when gently rolled between the hands.

	USA	Imperial	Metric
avocado, medium size	1	1	1
eggs	2	2	2
pineapple juice	2 tbsp	2 tbsp	28ml
double cream	10 fl oz	½ pint	284ml
sugar	2 tsp	2 tsp	2 tsp
pineapple slices	6	6	6

If you have an electric blender this can be made very simply by putting the peeled and sliced avocado into the blender with pineapple juice to purée, then adding the eggs. Whip cream with sugar until slightly thickened, then fold into avocado mixture. Pour into freezer tray and freeze for several hours, but remember to take it out to soften slightly before serving on well-drained and chilled pineapple slices.

Without a blender, peel and mash the avocado with a fork until smooth, add juice and beaten eggs. Fold into whipped cream and follow above directions.

New Orleans Cream Cheese Ice Cream (serves 6)

	USA	Imperial	Metric
cream cheese	½lb	8oz	200g
vanilla essence	½ tsp	½ tsp	½ tsp
salt	¼ tsp	¼ tsp	¼ tsp
walnuts, chopped	½ cup	2½oz	62½g
castor sugar	½ cup	4oz	100g
double cream	10 fl oz	½ pint	284ml

Mash cheese until very creamy, add vanilla, sugar, salt and nuts. Whip cream and fold into cheese mixture until well blended, pour into freezer tray and freeze.

Specially good served with chilled berries or sliced pineapple.

Instead of chopped nuts add same quantity of grated chocolate or chocolate pieces.

Fresh Strawberry Ice Cream (serves 6)

	USA	Imperial	Metric
strawberries	1¼lb	1¼lb	600g
sugar	½ cup	4oz	100g
water	4 tbsp	4 tbsp	56ml
lemon juice	1 tbsp	1 tbsp	1 tbsp
double cream	5 fl oz	¼ pint	142ml

Put berries into saucepan with sugar and water and crush slightly. Cook gently for 5 min. Cool, then put through fine sieve. Add lemon juice. Whip cream and fold into strawberry purée. Turn into freezer tray and freeze, stirring once or twice during freezing time.

Strawberry Water Ice (serves 6)

	USA	Imperial	Metric
strawberries	2lb	2lb	800g
lemon juice	1 tbsp	1 tbsp	1 tbsp
orange juice	2 tbsp	2 tbsp	28ml
sugar	1 cup	8oz	200g
water	5 fl oz	¼ pint	142ml

Boil sugar and water together for 5 min. When quite cold add to strawberries which have been pressed through a fine sieve. Add juices and mix well, then pour into freezer tray and freeze.

This should be served when well frozen.

Strawberry Sour Ice Cream (serves 6–8)

	USA	Imperial	Metric
strawberries	1lb	1lb	400g
dairy soured cream	2¼ cups	1 pint	568ml
castor sugar	½ cup	4oz	100g
brandy (optional)	2 tbsp	2 tbsp	28ml

Wash and hull strawberries, then place into blender with sugar and soured cream and blend until smooth. Add brandy if using. Without a blender press berries through sieve, then mix with soured cream and brandy. Pour into freezer tray and freeze, beating several times during freezing.

Raspberries are also delicious for this.

Berry Sorbet (serves 5–6)

Any berries, such as strawberries, raspberries, loganberries or gooseberries are good for this type of sorbet.

	USA	Imperial	Metric
berries	1lb	1lb	400g
water	10 fl oz	½ pint	284ml
sugar, to taste			
gelatine	1 tsp	1 tsp	1 tsp
egg whites	2	2	2

Cook berries in water with required amount of sugar for 5 min, crushing them gently. Press through a fine sieve, then dissolve gelatine in a little hot purée and blend in. Freeze until slightly thickened, turn into chilled bowl and beat, then fold in stiffly beaten egg whites and freeze again.

Purple plums also make a delicious sorbet with just a hint of tartness which is very refreshing. A blender makes preparations much simpler, but the plums will need a little longer cooking than the berries.

Tropical Freeze (serves 6)

	USA	Imperial	Metric
orange juice	10 fl oz	½ pint	284ml
lemon juice	5 fl oz	¼ pint	142ml
pineapple juice	10 fl oz	½ pint	284ml
orange rind, grated	1 tsp	1 tsp	1 tsp
sugar	1 cup	8oz	200g
double cream	10 fl oz	½ pint	284ml
gelatine	1 tsp	1 tsp	1 tsp
hot water	1 tbsp	1 tbsp	1 tbsp
pineapple cubes or slices			

Combine juices, peel and sugar and stir until sugar is dissolved. Dissolve gelatine in hot water and stir into juices. Whip cream until thick and fold juices into it until smooth. Pour into freezing tray and freeze, stirring once when half-frozen.

Serve on pineapple slices or garnish with pineapple cubes. Top with a sprig of fresh mint on each serving if available.

Orange Baskets

Choose required number of oranges all the same size and wash them well. Cut a thin slice from the top of each orange and carefully scrape out the pulp on to a plate. Remove as much white pith from inside each orange as possible without piercing the skins.

Chop up pulp after removing all pips and membranes, and blend this and the juice into plain vanilla ice cream which has slightly softened. Fill orange skins with this ice cream, replace tops as lids and put into freezing compartment until required. I find standing the oranges in plastic egg cartons keeps them upright in the refrigerator.

Instead of vanilla ice cream (either home-made or packaged) the orange baskets can be filled with either Tropical Freeze (p 163) or Berry Sorbet (p 162).

Tortoni (serves 6–8)

This delicious mixture can be made up and frozen in a loaf tin, then cut in slices to serve, or it can be divided between 6 or 8 foil cases (4½in, 11½cm size) and frozen.

Either home-made or commercially packaged ice cream can be used, as convenient.

	USA	Imperial	Metric
vanilla ice cream,			
large family block			
almond macaroon crumbs	*1 cup*	*¾ cup*	*200g*
cocktail cherries, chopped	*2 tbsp*	*2 tbsp*	*50g*
chopped nuts	*¼ cup*	*2oz*	*50g*
seedless raisins	*2 tbsp*	*2 tbsp*	*50g*
rum or sherry	*1 tbsp*	*1 tbsp*	*1 tbsp*

Pour boiling water over raisins and soak for 5 min, then drain and dry. Put into small basin and pour rum or sherry over them and leave for 1 hr. Mix macaroon crumbs, cherries, nuts and raisins together and blend with slightly softened—but not melted—ice cream. If using home-made ice cream, add the crumb mixture after the second beating. Turn into a loaf tin lined with a piece of foil long enough to hang over each side, and freeze. This makes it easier to remove ice cream from tin. Or freeze in foil cases for individual portions.

Cassata Bombe (serves 10–12)

Bombes make wonderful endings for dinner parties as they can be made up days beforehand and left in the freezing compartment of your refrigerator, or in a home freezer they will keep for several months.

They are usually made with several layers of different flavoured ice creams, with a creamy middle, and are best made in aluminium or plastic moulds shaped like a melon or plain round basins. Be sure to choose moulds which will fit into the freezing compartment, but if this is fairly shallow you could freeze the mixture in a square cake tin and cut it in slices to serve.

Either home-made or packaged ice cream can be used, but bombes are best made at least 2 days before serving.

STRAWBERRY BOMBE

	USA	Imperial	Metric
chocolate ice cream, large family block			
vanilla ice cream, large family block			
stale cake crumbs	¾ cup	¼ cup	40g
cherry brandy	1 tbsp	1 tbsp	1 tbsp
redcurrant jelly	2 tbsp	2 tbsp	50g
double cream	5 fl oz	¼ pint	142ml
castor sugar	1 tbsp	1 tbsp	1 tbsp
glacé cherries, chopped	6	6	6
blanched almonds, slivered	1 tbsp	1 tbsp	1 tbsp
candied peel, chopped	3 tsp	3 tsp	3 tsp
chocolate, grated	1 tbsp	1 tbsp	1 tbsp
almond essence	few drops	few drops	few drops

Soften chocolate ice cream slightly and spread over base and sides of 6½–7½ cup (2½–3 pint, 1½l) mould. Freeze until firm. Cover with layer of vanilla ice cream, leaving hollow in the centre. Mix cake crumbs, redcurrant jelly and cherry brandy together and spoon into hollow. Freeze until set. Whip cream until thick and add remainder of ingredients, then fill hollow completely, smoothing level at the top. Cover with a piece of foil and freeze bombe until ready to serve.

To remove bombe from mould wring out a cloth in hot water and put over the mould, which should be turned out on a well-chilled plate on which you have placed a paper doily. This prevents the bombe from slipping as it is cut in wedges to serve.

Strawberry Bombe (serves 8)

	USA	Imperial	Metric
strawberry ice cream (p 161)			
vanilla ice cream (p 158)			
double cream	5 fl oz	¼ pint	142ml
chopped nuts	1 tbsp	1 tbsp	1 tbsp

	USA	Imperial	Metric
seeded raisins, chopped	1 tbsp	1 tbsp	1 tbsp
glacé cherries, chopped	6	6	6
rum or brandy	2 tbsp	1 fl oz	28ml

Soak chopped cherries and raisins in brandy or rum for at least 1 hr. Line a 4 cup (1½–2 pint, 1l) mould with strawberry ice cream and freeze. Pack over this a layer of vanilla ice cream, leaving a hollow in the centre. Freeze. Whip cream and fold in chopped nuts, cherries and raisins and the liquor they were soaked in. Pack this into the hollow in the mould, levelling off the top. Cover with a piece of foil and freeze until required. Serve as above.

Christmas Bombe (serves 8–10)

This is a wonderful dessert for a Christmas party, and is all the better for being made and frozen at least a week before serving. Garnish it with a sprig of holly and serve whipped cream separately.

When we lived in Australia, where Christmas temperatures are sometimes up sky-high, a cold dinner, with turkey and salads, was often finished with this ice cream Christmas pudding, but it can also be just as good at any other time of the year.

	USA	Imperial	Metric
chocolate ice cream, family block			
vanilla ice cream, family block			
fruit mincemeat	1lb jar	1lb jar	400g jar
brandy, rum or lemon juice	1 tbsp	1 tbsp	1 tbsp
gingernut biscuits, crushed	¼ cup	2oz	50g

Blend brandy, rum or lemon juice with fruit mincemeat and allow to stand for 1 hr. Line a basin with a layer of chocolate ice cream and freeze. Blend half the vanilla ice cream with fruit mincemeat and pack over the chocolate layer, leaving a hollow in the middle. Freeze. Blend gingernut crumbs into remainder of vanilla ice cream and pack into hollow of mould, levelling off the top. Cover with foil and freeze until required.

Bombe Alaska (serves 6–8)

Many a hostess has known the anxious moment of serving an ice cream dessert too soon, then to watch her guests chattering round the table as the ice cream melts slowly into a puddle on their plates.

Because of this many hesitate to try a Bombe Alaska, or its companion, Baked Alaska, thinking that only professional chefs can be brave enough to put such a fragile dessert into the oven. But if a few simple rules are followed these delicious 'endings' to a good dinner can be made by even novice cooks, and because I have found that an hour in the freezer before serving improves the Alaska, it can even be made by those who have no help in the kitchen for last-minute serving.

First, the cake which is the base for either of the Alaskas, and the covered board on which it stands in the oven, must initially be thoroughly chilled.

Then the ice cream shape must be frozen solid.

The meringue must be ready at the same time as the cake and ice cream so they are not kept waiting, and the oven must be at the right temperature.

Care must be taken that the meringue covers the cake and ice cream completely and evenly.

It is important to select a bread board of a size that will not only fit into the oven, but also into the freezing compartment of your refrigerator or your home freezer. This board should be at least 2in (5cm) wider than the diameter of the sponge cake you are using. If you haven't a suitable melon-shaped mould for the ice cream use a plastic or aluminium basin in which to freeze it for the Bombe Alaska, but for Baked Alaska a square or rectangular cake and ice cream block is used, although both are prepared in the same way.

8in (20cm) round sponge cake
large carton ice cream
basic meringue mixture (p 151)

Cover bread board with aluminium foil. Place cake on board and chill for 1 hr. Soften ice cream slightly and pack into 6in (15cm) mould or basin, and freeze until solid. Prepare meringue.

Take chilled board and cake from freezer, run a knife or spatula round mould, turn upside-down over cake so ice cream turns out precisely in centre of cake. Working quickly, swirl meringue over ice cream and cake with a flexible spatula, making sure it is completely sealed to the board. Put into a very hot oven (450° F, 230° C, Gas Mark 8) for 5 min or until meringue is tinted a pale golden. Serve at once, or put into freezer for 1 hr, then serve cut in slices.

Bombe Vesuvius (serves 6–8)

Follow the directions for Bombe Alaska, but use chocolate ice cream. The sponge base may be sprinkled with a little rum if liked, but don't make it soggy. When covering with meringue shape it into a peak on the top to resemble a mountain. Bake as directed, then put into freezer for about 1 hr.

Just before serving lightly press half an eggshell into the peak (making sure it is quite dry inside); sprinkle 2 cubes of loaf sugar with lemon essence and stand in egg shell, then set them alight. Take to the table at once while still blazing.

Another version of this recipe which is very popular for special occasions in Italy follows the above directions, but just after taking from freezer hot melted chocolate is dribbled down the sides of the meringue to resemble lava. It is then flamed as above and quickly taken to the table to be served.

Strawberry Alaska Pie (serves 6)

Marvellous for when strawberries are in season, or other fruit such as canned peaches or pineapple can be used in the same recipe.

	USA	Imperial	Metric
shortcrust pastry case (p 172)			
strawberries	1lb	1lb	400g
vanilla ice cream, family block			
egg whites	3	3	3

	USA	Imperial	Metric
castor sugar	6 tbsp	6 tbsp	150g
cornflour	1 tsp	1 tsp	1 tsp
salt	pinch	pinch	pinch

Make up an 8in (20cm) pastry case as directed on page 171, baking it in an ovenproof dish suitable for serving at table. This can be made up the day before and stored when cold in an air-tight container.

Hull the berries, and put aside 6 or 8 of the largest and best for garnishing. Arrange remainder in the pie shell. Allow ice cream to soften very slightly, then spoon it over the berries, covering them completely, but leaving the pastry edging uncovered, and mounding ice cream up in the middle. Place pie in freezer or freezing section of refrigerator until nearly serving time.

Beat egg whites until stiff and dry, then beat in sugar gradually until completely dissolved. Add cornflour with the last of the sugar. Spread this meringue over the pie, sealing well to the inside edge of the pastry, and rough up the top with a fork. Place pie on a bread board covered in foil and put into a very hot oven (450° F, 230° C, Gas Mark 8) for 5 min, until meringue is set.

This can be put back into the freezer for up to 1 hr if more convenient, or served at once. Use strawberries which were put aside to garnish round the edge of the pie.

Cream can be served with this if desired, but it is not really necessary.

Pastries & Pies

MAKING THE PASTRY

Flaky, golden crusted pies, filled with fish, meat, fruits or some other sweet mixture are always popular items on the menu. There are a number of different types of pastry, all having their own particular place when planning meals for family or guests.

The secret of making good pastry, whichever type you are making, is in the handling of the dough. The less it is handled the lighter the pastry will be when baked. Another important point is to have all ingredients as cold as possible—work in a cool place, and have all the utensils chilled before using. The best pastry maker I know uses a plain bottle filled with ice water for rolling out her pastry.

Pastry can be made with a variety of fats such as butter, lard, white vegetable shortening or margarine, or a mixture of margarine and butter, or lard and butter.

Various flavourings can be added to the pastry, for instance for meat pies add a little curry powder or dry mustard to the flour, and for dessert pies add grated orange or lemon rind, or a little spice such as nutmeg or cinnamon. Finely chopped nuts are also good blended into short pastry.

When making a top-and-bottom pie, divide the pastry into 2 portions, rolling firmly, quickly and evenly to required thickness. Support the pastry over the rolling pin as you lift it from the board to the pie dish or pie plate. Remove the rolling pin carefully and smooth the pastry down with your fingers, being careful not to stretch the pastry and making sure there are no air bubbles underneath. An inverted cup or a pastry funnel can be placed in the centre of a deep pie dish to support the pastry if necessary.

If a double edge is wanted, cut the top pastry about 1in (2½cm) larger all round than the pie dish and double it under the pastry lining, crimping the edges together with a fork or by pressing between the thumb and first finger all round. If a single edge is wanted, moisten the edge of the lower crust before covering with the top, then cut off surplus pastry, and crimp edges.

If a recipe says to 'bake blind' it means that the pastry case is baked without being filled. In order to prevent the pastry base from rising as it cooks it should be lined on the bottom with greased cooking foil or greaseproof paper, then covered with dried beans, rice or bread crusts (the crusts can be rolled out afterwards for breadcrumbs). Bake the case for about 15 min, then remove the filling and the paper and continue baking until pastry is cooked. The beans or rice may be stored and used time and time again for the same purpose.

A flan case is made with a special flan ring, which is placed on a baking tin or tray turned upside-down (this makes it easier to remove flan after baking). Roll out the pastry into a circle about 1½in (4cm) larger than the ring, support it over the rolling pin and lower into the flan ring, remove pin and press pastry on to the base and round the sides without stretching it. Roll the pin over the top of the flan and the surplus pastry will be cut away.

METRIC MEASUREMENTS

As I have used an approximate equivalent in this book of 25g to 1oz to make conversions more simple, some of the measurements you are accustomed to using—ie 8oz flour being just enough for your particular pie dish—you will find that pastry made with 200g flour will not be enough.

So I have used 225g flour to 113g fat which is nearer the exact conversion, and still retains the correct proportions for short pastry of half fat to flour. The proportions for flaky pastry are two-thirds fat to flour, and puff pastry is equal amounts of fat and flour.

When a recipe calls for 8oz pastry, this means pastry made with 8oz (225g) flour plus the fat and any other ingredients, which gives a total weight of about 12oz (340g).

Pastry freezes well, either cooked or uncooked. After making as directed form pastry into a square, wrap in polythene bag or in cooking foil, label with date and weight, and freeze. If more convenient the pastry can be rolled out and used to line aluminium foil pie plates or tart cases, then frozen. These can be taken straight from the freezer and baked. If pastry is frozen after being made up into sausage rolls, Cornish pasties or meat pies, it is best to allow them to defrost before baking or the fillings may not be heated through.

An electric beater can be used for blending the fat into the flour for short pastry, but care should be taken not to over-beat.

Shortcrust Pastry

	USA	Imperial	Metric
self-raising flour	2 cups	8oz	200g or 225g (see above)
fat	½ cup	4oz	100g or 115g (see above)
salt	½ tsp	½ tsp	½ tsp
water	2 tbsp (approx)	2 tbsp	2 tbsp

Sift flour and salt into mixing bowl and rub in fat until mixture is like fine breadcrumbs. Add water gradually, mixing lightly with a round-topped knife. The mixture is the right consistency when the sides of the bowl are clean. Turn out on a lightly floured board, shape quickly into a ball, then roll out to required shape with lightly floured rolling pin.

Rich Short Pastry (Sweet)

Make as above but sift in 2 tbsp icing sugar with the flour and mix with
1 egg yolk and 1–2 tsp water as required. Chill for a time before rolling
out.

Cheese Pastry

Make as for shortcrust pastry but use only 3oz (75g) fat. Add 2oz
(50g) grated cheese and ½ tsp dry mustard, and mix either with water
or with an egg yolk and water.

Flaky Pastry

This pastry takes longer to make than the shortcrust as it should be
'rested' in the refrigerator or a cold place for at least 20 min between
each folding to firm the fat, and also before baking.

	USA	*Imperial*	*Metric*
plain flour	*2 cups*	*8oz*	*200g or 225g (see above)*
salt	*¼ tsp*	*¼ tsp*	*¼ tsp*
fat	*¾ cup*	*6oz*	*150g or 175g (see above)*
water, iced, to mix			
lemon juice	*2 tsp*	*2 tsp*	*2 tsp*

Sift flour and salt into a bowl. Divide fat into 3 portions, and rub 1
portion into flour. Mix to a good consistency with iced water and
lemon juice, turn out and knead lightly until smooth on a floured
board. Cover with foil or polythene and put into refrigerator to rest.

Roll out to an oblong shape, cut second portion of fat into flakes
and place them evenly on two-thirds of the dough, using a flexible
spatula or wide-bladed knife. Fold into 3, folding plain side over first.
Press edges together and roll again into an oblong, but turning at
right angles before rolling. Put into refrigerator to rest again, then
repeat the same process with remaining fat, and chill before baking.

This amount will make 2 8in (20cm) flan cases or an 8in (20cm)
double-crust pie.

Rough Puff Pastry

This is somewhat similar to flaky pastry, but is simpler to make. It can be used for any recipes calling for flaky pastry. Ingredients are same as flaky pastry in above recipe.

Sift flour and salt in bowl. Cut fat into small pieces and add to flour, mixing well, then add water and lemon juice to mix to a fairly stiff dough. Turn out on a lightly floured board and roll out to an oblong. Fold and roll as in flaky pastry, resting in the refrigerator between rollings. Chill well before rolling out for the last time.

Choux Pastry

Entirely different from the pastries given above, this is made in a saucepan, and needs no rolling out. Choux pastry is used for making cream puffs and eclairs, and should puff up to about 3 times its original size after baking. The oven temperature is important if the pastry is to hold its shape, and the oven should not be opened for the first 15 min baking at 400° F, 200° C, Gas Mark 6, then it should be lowered to 375° F, 190° C, Gas Mark 5 for 15–20 min. The baked pastry should be cooled away from draughts to prevent falling.

	USA	Imperial	Metric
butter	2 tbsp	1oz	25g
water	9 tbsp	$\frac{1}{4}$ pint	142ml
flour	$\frac{3}{4}$ cup	3oz	75g or 85g
salt	$\frac{1}{4}$ tsp	$\frac{1}{4}$ tsp	$\frac{1}{4}$ tsp
eggs	2	2	2
egg yolk	1	1	1

Sift flour and salt on to a plate. Put butter and water into saucepan and heat until butter has melted and water is boiling. Remove from heat and add flour all at once, stirring until well blended, using a wooden spoon. Return to heat and cook very slowly, stirring all the time, until you have a smooth dry ball which leaves the sides of the pan clean. Remove from heat and beat in eggs one at a time, lastly beating in only as much of the egg yolk as needed to make a smooth mixture firm enough to hold soft peaks when lifted with a spoon.

Cream Puffs: Using above pastry, spoon or pipe rounds of size desired on a greased and floured baking tray. Bake in centre of moderately hot oven for 15 min, then lower heat and continue cooking for 15–20 min. Cool away from draughts, split through the middle and carefully remove any uncooked dough in the centre. Allow to dry out for a little time, then fill with desired filling.

These can be filled and just heated through in a moderate oven if wanted to serve hot.

Country Apple Pie (serves 6)

	USA	Imperial	Metric
shortcrust pastry (p 172)	2 cups	8oz	225g
cooking apples, large	5–6	5–6	5–6
butter, melted	2 tbsp	2 tbsp	2 tbsp
egg, large	1	1	1
flour	2 tbsp	2 tbsp	2 tbsp
sugar	1 cup	8oz	200g
salt	pinch	pinch	pinch
cinnamon, ground	1 tsp	1 tsp	1 tsp
lemon juice	2 tsp	2 tsp	2 tsp
cream	¾ cup	6 fl oz	170ml
milk	1 tbsp	1 tbsp	1 tbsp

Roll out pastry to ⅛in (⅓cm) thickness and line a deep 9in (23cm) pie plate, keeping aside remainder of pastry to cover filling. Peel, core and slice apples and arrange in pie shell. Combine all remaining ingredients except milk, beating together well, then pour over apples. Cover with remaining pastry, trim, turn edge under and flute the edge, then cut a few vents in the top crust. Cut out leaves to decorate top and brush pastry over with milk. Bake in a fairly hot oven (400° F, 200° C, Gas Mark 6) for 50 min to 1 hr, until pastry is golden and apples are cooked.

Serve hot.

Apple Meringue Pie (serves 6)

	USA	Imperial	Metric
shortcrust pastry (p 172)	*2 cups*	*8oz*	*225g*
eggs	*2*	*2*	*2*
lemon rind, grated	*1 tbsp*	*1 tbsp*	*1 tbsp*
cooking apples	*2lb*	*2lb*	*800g*
castor sugar	*1 tbsp*	*1 tbsp*	*1 tbsp*
granulated sugar	*2 tbsp*	*2 tbsp*	*2 tbsp*

Make up short pastry as directed on page 172, adding 1 tsp grated lemon rind, 1 tbsp castor sugar and use yolk of egg to mix. Roll out carefully about ⅛in (¾cm) thick and line a well-greased 9in (23cm) pie dish, making a double edge round the dish, and crimping together.

Cook the peeled, cored and sliced apples with very little water, keeping them as dry as possible. When cooked add 1 tbsp granulated sugar, remainder of lemon rind and 1 beaten egg yolk, beating all together until mixture is smooth. Pour into pastry-lined dish and bake in moderately hot oven (400° F, 200° C, Gas Mark 6) for 10 min, then reduce heat to fairly moderate (325° F, 160° C, Gas Mark 3) and continue cooking until pastry is cooked through and golden, about another 20 min. Remove from oven.

Beat egg whites until stiff, then beat in remainder of sugar. Spread over apples, taking meringue right to the edge of apples, and roughing up the top. Put back into oven long enough to crisp meringue and tint pale golden.

Serve hot or cold.

Apple and Pineapple Meringue Pie (serves 6)
Follow above directions but substitute well-drained canned crushed pineapple for half the cooked apples.

French Apple Flan (serves 4–5)
In the country districts of France village housewives still take their baking to be cooked in the oven of the local baker after he has finished

his bread. I have frequently seen women walking through the streets—
especially on Sunday mornings—carrying large open fruit pies to the
baker, some of these pies being 12in to 14in across, and they look and
smell delicious after baking. This is the same type of pie, but made in a
smaller version for smaller ovens.

	USA	Imperial	Metric
shortcrust pastry (p 172)	8oz	8oz	225g
tart eating apples	3–4	3–4	3–4
glacé cherries	3	3	3
castor sugar	4 tbsp	4 tbsp	4 tbsp
white wine or lemon juice	2 tbsp	2 tbsp	2 tbsp
apricot jam	4 tbsp	4 tbsp	4 tbsp
lemon juice	2 tbsp	2 tbsp	2 tbsp

Roll pastry out thinly and line a shallow 7in (18cm) flan ring or
loose-bottomed sandwich tin, taking care not to stretch dough. Trim
round the edges and prick base with a fork. Peel, core and slice apples
evenly, keeping slices as nearly the same size as possible.

Starting from the outside edge and working into the centre, arrange
the slices in a spiral with each one overlapping the preceding one until
the flan is entirely filled. Finish the centre with the glacé cherries.
Sprinkle with the castor sugar and white wine or lemon juice. Bake in
a fairly hot oven (400° F, 200° C, Gas Mark 6) for about 20 min, or
until the pastry is golden brown and apples just cooked.

Make a glaze with the apricot jam, 2 tbsp lemon juice and 1 tbsp
water, stirring over low heat until dissolved, stirring all the time. Boil
briskly for a few minutes until slightly thick. Rub this through a sieve
or put through an electric blender, then spoon it evenly over the
apples, taking it right to the edge of the flan to give a good finish.

Serve hot or cold with cream or custard, or it is nice just as it is.

Orange Custard Tart (serves 4–5)

	USA	Imperial	Metric
rich short pastry (p 173)	6oz	6oz	150g
orange rind, grated	1 heaped tbsp	1 heaped tbsp	1 heaped tbsp
milk	1¼ cups	½ pint	284ml
eggs	3	3	3
castor sugar	2 tbsp	1oz	25g
grated nutmeg, to taste			
salt	pinch	pinch	pinch

Roll pastry out into a circle and line a deep 8in (20cm) pie plate. Trim and flute edges of pastry. Separate white and yolk of 1 egg and brush over base of pie with the lightly beaten egg white, and allow to dry before filling with the custard.

Add yolk to other 2 eggs in a bowl and beat lightly together with the sugar and salt. Heat milk until just luke-warm and beat into eggs. Add orange rind and pour mixture into pastry-lined pie plate. Sprinkle top with nutmeg.

Stand pie plate on baking tray and put into a moderate oven (350° F, 180° C, Gas Mark 4). Bake for 45–50 min until custard is set and pastry is golden brown. Serve hot or cold.

The grated orange rind may be omitted if plain custard is preferred.

Florida Pie (serves 4–5)

An unusual filling for a pie which is a real taste treat. Either fresh or canned citrus fruit can be used, but fresh fruit will need the addition of sugar while the canned variety is usually quite sweet enough.

1 cup grapefruit segments
1 cup orange segments
1 cup drained canned pineapple pieces

1 tbsp pineapple juice
rich short pastry (p 173), 8oz (200g or 225g)
castor sugar, to taste

Roll out pastry into a circle to fit over a 5 cup (2 pint, 1¼ litre) lipped pie dish, leaving a good border all round. Cut a strip of pastry to fit round edge of dish. Moisten edge of dish with water and press strip in place. Mix the fruit together with juice, add sugar if needed, and fill dish, then cover with pastry, being careful not to stretch it. Trim edge and flute. Make a small hole in top of pastry, and trim with pastry leaves, then brush over with milk. Bake in a hot oven (425° F, 220° C, Gas Mark 7) for 15 min, then reduce heat to moderate for 25 min.

Black Bottom Pie (serves 5–6)

This is a recipe I collected from one of my hostesses when in Missouri, and find it is always popular.

	USA	Imperial	Metric
dark block chocolate	*8oz*	*8oz*	*200g*
custard	*2¼ cups*	*1 pint*	*568ml*
whipping cream	*¼ cup*	*4oz*	*113ml*
shortcrust pastry (p 172)	*6oz*	*6oz*	*150g*

Roll out pastry and line an 8in (20cm) pie plate. Prick lightly with a fork and line with foil or greaseproof paper, keeping this down with some stale crusts or dried beans. Bake in hot oven (425° F, 220° C, Gas Mark 7) for 15 min, then remove filling and return to oven for a further 10 min until pastry is golden brown.

Grate the chocolate and sprinkle 6oz (150g) over the base of the hot pastry shell immediately after it comes from the oven. If this is not possible, melt the chocolate and spread over the pastry. Put aside to cool and set. Make up custard (this can be made with custard powder) and when quite cool pour over chocolate in pastry shell. Chill until ready to serve, then cover with whipped cream and sprinkle with remaining grated chocolate.

Baklava (serves 8)

This is a sweet, nut-filled pastry which is found all over the Balkans. The Turks will tell you they invented it, and in Greece they will tell you it is a typical Greek sweet—but whoever made it first doesn't really matter, for it is obtainable in both countries and well worth trying.

But home cooks will find it comes out somewhat different, because the phyllo pastry with which it is made is almost impossible for any but a Balkan professional—but I make it with packaged puff pastry bought from the supermarket and haven't had any complaints about it yet.

It is a sweet, rich pastry, so small helpings are advised. Either walnuts or almonds can be used, or a mixture of both.

	USA	Imperial	Metric
puff pastry	1 lb	1 lb	400 g
butter	½ cup	4 oz	100 g
flaked almonds	1 cup	4 oz	100 g
granulated sugar	½ cup	4 oz	100 g
clear honey	1 lb	1 lb	400 g
ground cinnamon	1 tsp	1 tsp	1 tsp
lemon juice	1 tsp	1 tsp	1 tsp
hot water	½ cup	4 fl oz	113 ml

Divide the pastry into 4 portions and roll out as thinly as possible, without breaking it, into rectangles about 12in × 8in (30cm × 20cm), to fit a Swiss roll tin which should be brushed over with melted butter. Place a layer of pastry in the tin, brush this generously with melted butter then sprinkle with a mixture of nuts and cinnamon. Repeat these layers until all the pastry is used up, ending with a topping of nuts and cinnamon. If you are clever enough with a rolling pin to get 5 sheets of pastry use it on top.

With a sharp knife cut the layers lengthwise through the centre without taking through to the bottom layer, then mark into squares of serving size. Bake in a hot oven (425° F, 220° C, Gas Mark 7) for 15 min, then reduce heat to moderate for a further 35–40 min, until cooked and golden. Cool.

Make a syrup by dissolving the sugar in the water, then boil rapidly for 5 min without stirring. Add honey and lemon juice and just bring to the boil. Place the Baklava on a serving dish and pour syrup over it while still boiling, covering it well. Allow to cool before serving, by which time the syrup should be almost absorbed into the pastry.

CRUMB CRUSTS

An alternative to pastry is to make crumb crusts, which can be used with either sweet or savoury fillings, depending on the crumbs used. These are particularly useful for hot weather meals, as they require no cooking, but should be prepared some hours beforehand and well chilled before filling and serving.

It is important that the crumbs should be crushed evenly, and this can be done by putting the biscuits or crackers into a brown paper bag and crushing them with a rolling pin, or using an electric blender.

Cornflakes also make a good crust when crushed fine, and other ingredients you can use for these crusts are quick-cooking porridge oats, coconut or oven-browned breadcrumbs. You can use butter, margarine or white vegetable shortening.

Biscuit Crumb Crust

	USA	Imperial	Metric
fine biscuit crumbs	1½ cups	6oz	150g
butter or margarine, melted	½ cup	4oz	100g
sugar	¼ cup	2oz	50g

Crush the crumbs evenly and blend with the melted butter and sugar. Press evenly and firmly over the base and sides of an 8in (20cm) pie plate or flan ring. Chill well for about 1 hr, then fill with preferred mixture.

SPICED CRUMB PIE SHELL

Spiced Crumb Pie Shell

This is a good way of using up stale bread. The bread should be cut thin and baked in the oven until golden brown and crisp. When cold the bread is crushed into fine crumbs. These can then be used in place of biscuit crumbs as in the preceding recipe, and 1 tsp ground cinnamon and ½ tsp ground nutmeg added to the mixture.

For a filling use packaged caramel or butterscotch dessert, adding 2 tsp gelatine dissolved in a little water. Allow to cool but not set before pouring into the crumb shell. Chill before serving.

Crunchy Orange Pie Shell

	USA	Imperial	Metric
cornflakes, crushed	1¼ cups	6oz	150g
orange rind, grated	2 tsp	2 tsp	2 tsp
sugar	¼ cup	2oz	50g
butter, melted	½ cup	4oz	100g

Blend all together and press evenly round the sides and base of a well-buttered 8in (20cm) pie plate or flan ring. Chill well for about 30 min.

This is very good filled with ice cream.

There are more recipes for flans and tarts in other sections of this book. See Index.

Hot Puddings

PUDDINGS WITH APPLES

History tells us that the Romans first planted apple trees in Britain, and apple trees have been flourishing there ever since. When the early colonists left for America they took both apple seeds and cuttings with them and soon fine European apples were giving splendid crops in all the settlements.

A story I always enjoy tells of Johnny Appleseed, as he was known, who had a good orchard near the Eastern American coast but left it to follow the frontiersmen who were opening up the West. Everywhere he went he planted apple seeds in order that those pioneers who followed him would find apples growing to give them a familiar fruit from home. He became a legend in his own lifetime, and it is said that many a weary traveller decided to settle where he found some of Johnny Appleseed's trees growing, and these became the nuclei of many excellent farms.

Australia, too, owes the beginning of its fine orchards to the early settlers who took English apple seeds and cuttings with them to the new land where they were to make their future homes. One apple which is known today all over the world, the splendid Granny Smith, which I consider is just as good for eating as it is for cooking, owes its discovery to an old lady in Western Australia, after whom it is named.

The warm, spicy smell of an apple pie baking is one of the most delicious smells I know, and although few of us today make the variety of pies which were once expected from every good housewife, an apple pie 'like mother used to make' never loses its popularity. You may serve your pie with cheese or with cream, flavoured with mixed spice or cloves, combine the apples with rhubarb or blackberries, just as you please—such an ending to a meal is always a good one. See recipes on page 175.

Another old-fashioned way of cooking apples is to bake them, and this simple dish can be served without any apologies at a dinner party just as well as at a family meal. Or there are apple dumplings, which, like baked apples, can be filled with a wide variety of different mixtures to make them taste different every time they are served.

But the number of ways you can cook apples is too numerous to mention here, and there is space for only a few which are my favourites —and I hope will be yours after you have tried them.

Many Continental countries, especially France and Italy, serve fresh fruit to end the meal, and a basket of fruit, particularly apples in season, often does double duty as both a table decoration and a dessert.

And what could be more attractive after a good dinner than a basket or wooden platter of assorted apples, using a mixture of bright red apples such as Jonathans, Laxton's Superb or Red Delicious, green Granny Smith's, and Golden Delicious, the mixture of colours adding to the interest. Serve them just slightly chilled, well polished and garnished with fresh green leaves.

Apples and cheese are another popular ending, the two blending well together, and a wooden platter centred with a pyramid of rosy apples and encircled with an assortment of cheeses is both decorative and very acceptable as a happy ending.

For details of cheeses see pages 213–15.

BAKED APPLES

Bramley's or Grannie Smith's are good for this method of cooking. Choose large apples, all the same size so they will cook at the same time, and watch them carefully so they do not split. Basting them as they bake gives them a nice glaze.

A variety of fillings can be used for apples such as are given in the following recipes.

Wash the apples well and remove cores, then make a slight cut through the skin round the centre of each apple. Rub over skin with buttered paper and place apples in a fairly deep ovenproof dish which can be brought to the table for serving. Fill centres with any of the following mixtures and bake in a fairly slow oven (325° F, 160° C, Gas Mark 3) for 1–1½ hr, depending on size. Baste occasionally with juices in the dish. They are usually best served hot.

Spiced Apples (serves 4)

	USA	Imperial	Metric
butter	¼ cup	2oz	50g
brown sugar	½ cup	4oz	100g
ground cinnamon	¼ tsp	¼ tsp	¼ tsp
ground ginger	¼ tsp	¼ tsp	¼ tsp
seedless raisins, chopped	½ cup	2oz	50g

Cream butter and sugar together with spices, add raisins and fill apple centres with this mixture. Place in baking dish and add ¼ cup hot water to dish. Bake as directed above.

Christmas Mincemeat Apples

These are good to make if there is any mincemeat left from Christmas —but they are just as nice at any other time.

Fill each prepared apple with 1 tbsp of fruit mincemeat, top each with 1 tsp butter, and add either cider, port wine or orange juice to the baking dish.

Serve each apple topped with a spoonful of sour cream for a piquant flavour.

Or make a meringue topping as given on page 176 and when apples are baked and slightly cooled, cover with meringue, return to a slow oven to set and just lightly tint the meringue. Serve at once.

Apples Arabic (serves 4)

	USA	Imperial	Metric
whole dates	12	12	12
ginger in syrup	2oz	2oz	50g
sugar	4 tsp	4 tsp	4 tsp
orange rind, grated	1 tbsp	1 tbsp	1 tbsp
orange juice	¾ cup	6 fl oz	170ml
cooking apples	4	4	4

Prepare apples as above. Remove stones from dates and insert a piece of ginger in each. Mix sugar and grated orange rind together. Fill apples with alternate dates and sugar mixture, place in baking dish. Add a little ginger syrup (depending on taste) to the orange juice and pour round the apples. Bake in a moderate oven (350° F, 180° C, Gas Mark 4) for about 45–50 min, or until tender but unbroken.

For those who prefer a rather tart flavour, substitute lemon instead of orange rind, and use half lemon and half orange juice.

Baked Apples Hawaii (serves 4)

The rum in this recipe adds a very good flavour, but it can be omitted if preferred.

	USA	Imperial	Metric
tart cooking apples	4 large	4 large	4 large
canned pineapple slices	6	6	6
butter	2 tbsp	2oz	50g
light brown sugar	2 tbsp	2oz	50g
oil or margarine	2 tbsp	2 tbsp	2 tbsp
pineapple juice	2 tbsp	2 tbsp	2 tbsp
rum	1 tbsp	1 tbsp	1 tbsp
shredded coconut	2 tbsp	2 tbsp	2 tbsp

Choose apples all the same size if possible. Remove cores and peel about a quarter of the way down each apple. Stand in a deep buttered casserole. Crush 2 slices well-drained pineapple to a pulp, or put through blender. Cream butter and sugar together and add to crushed pineapple. Fill apples with this mixture, spreading over tops as well. Add rum and pineapple juice round the apples, cover casserole and bake in a moderate oven (350° F, 180° C, Gas Mark 4) until apples are tender but unbroken, for about 1 hr. Remove cover and sprinkle coconut over the top of apples and replace in oven just until coconut is golden.

Meanwhile, heat oil or margarine or a mixture of both in a large frying pan and lightly fry drained pineapple slices on both sides. Remove to a serving dish and place an apple on each pineapple slice, then pour syrup from casserole round them.

Serve hot.

Jamaican Apples

Very similar to the above, but the apples are filled with a mixture of crushed pineapple and apricot jam, and basted frequently with pineapple juice and rum during the baking time to give a good glaze.

They should be served hot with thick cream.

Apple and Orange Brown Betty (serves 6)

This is a recipe I collected from the wife of a fruit farmer who was camping in Yellowstone Park when we were there also. She had the most marvellous assortment of recipes, several of which I have used in this book, and was very thrilled to receive some of my English and Continental recipes in exchange—which is a good way of making friends everywhere.

	USA	Imperial	Metric
tart cooking apples	6	6	6
orange juice	½ cup	4 fl oz	113ml
sugar	¼ cup	2oz	50g
ground nutmeg	½ tsp	½ tsp	½ tsp
wholemeal digestive biscuits	16	16	16
soft brown sugar	½ cup	4oz	100g

	USA	Imperial	Metric
orange rind, grated	2 tsp	2 tsp	2 tsp
walnuts or hazelnuts, chopped	¼ cup	1oz	12½g
butter or margarine	½ cup	4oz	100g

Peel, core and quarter apples and cook with orange juice until just tender. Add sugar and nutmeg and place in shallow ovenproof dish. Crush biscuits to coarse crumbs, mix with brown sugar, grated rind, nuts and butter and sprinkle over apples. Bake in moderate oven (375° F, 190° C, Gas Mark 5) until topping is crunchy.

Apple Cheese Crumble (serves 4–5)

This can be made in a pre-baked pie shell or the apples can be put into an ovenproof pie dish and covered with the topping, just as you please.

	USA	Imperial	Metric
cooking apples	3 large	3 large	3 large
lemon juice or cider	1 tbsp	1 tbsp	1 tbsp
ground cinnamon	1 tsp	1 tsp	1 tsp
light brown sugar	1 tbsp	1oz	25g
flour	1 cup	4oz	100g
butter or margarine	3 tbsp	1½oz	37½g
granulated sugar	2 tbsp	2oz	50g
cheese, grated	½ cup	2oz	50g

Peel, core and slice apples and cook with the lemon juice or cider, brown sugar and cinnamon until soft. Turn into an ovenproof pie dish or a baked pastry shell and cool.

Make the topping by blending together flour, butter or margarine, sugar and grated cheese until mixture resembles coarse breadcrumbs. Sprinkle this evenly over the apples.

Bake in a moderate oven (350° F, 180° C, Gas Mark 4) until topping is slightly crisp and golden brown, about 30–35 min.

Serve hot.

Apples with Macaroon Topping (serves 4–5)
Another version of the above recipe.

	USA	Imperial	Metric
cooked apples as in above recipe			
egg whites	2 large	2 large	2 large
castor sugar	½ cup	4oz	100g
ground almonds	½ cup	2oz	50g
almond essence	few drops		

Whip egg whites until light and fluffy. Fold in other ingredients, mixing well but lightly, and pile roughly over the apples in an oven-proof pie dish.

Bake in a fairly slow oven (325° F, 160° C, Gas Mark 3) for about 25 min, until top is pale golden, and crisp.

Apple Almond Crumble (serves 4–5)
Another topping for cooked apples.

	USA	Imperial	Metric
flour	¾ cup	3oz	75g
Demerara sugar	3 tbsp	3oz	75g
butter or margarine	6 tbsp	3oz	75g
ground almonds	½ cup	2oz	50g

Blend all together and sprinkle evenly over the apples in a pie dish. Bake in moderate oven (350° F, 180° C, Gas Mark 4) for about 30–35 min.

Glazed Apple Rings (serves 4)
Two versions of this simple dish—one for special occasions and the other for everyday meals.

	USA	Imperial	Metric
cooking apples	2 large	2 large	2 large
butter or margarine	2 tbsp	1oz	25g

	USA	Imperial	Metric
castor sugar	¼ cup	2oz	50g
golden syrup or honey	3 tbsp	3 tbsp	3 tbsp
soft breadcrumbs	1 cup	2oz	50g

Peel and core apples, slice across into 4 thick rings (the top and bottom slices of each apple can be used for something else). Melt butter or margarine in a large frying pan or baking dish, melt sugar and syrup or honey, stirring to prevent burning, and cook apple slices gently in this for about 15–20 min, turning carefully halfway through cooking time, until fruit is tender but unbroken.

Using a wide spatula or fish slice, remove slices from pan, and place each one in an individual sweet dish.

Put the breadcrumbs into the syrup in the pan (adding a little more butter if necessary) and stir gently over low heat until crisp. Sprinkle over top of apple slices and serve with cream or custard.

For a special occasion, omit the breadcrumbs, top each with a scoop of ice cream and cover with syrup.

Danish Apple Pudding (serves 6)

This is a delicious pudding, known in Denmark by the delightful name of 'Peasant Girl with a Veil'.

	USA	Imperial	Metric
cooking apples	1¼lb	1¼lb	600g
brown breadcrumbs	2 cups	4oz	100g
butter	2 tbsp	1oz	25g
granulated sugar	2 tbsp	2oz	50g
dark chocolate	2 squares	2oz	50g
whipping cream	¼ cup	5 fl oz	142ml

Peel, core and slice apples and cook gently in a very little water until soft. While apples are cooking prepare the breadcrumbs. Melt butter in a fairly large baking dish, add breadcrumbs and sugar, mixing all together. Place in fairly hot oven until crumbs are crisp and brown, stirring occasionally and be sure crumbs don't burn.

When apples are cooked beat them until smooth or put through an electric blender. Put a layer of crisp crumbs in a serving dish, then a layer of apples, repeating these layers until all ingredients are used, finishing with a layer of crumbs. Chill well.

Just before serving beat cream until thick, and pile on top of pudding. Grate the chocolate and add to top of cream.

Apricot Almond Crumble (serves 6)

Try this elegant dessert when you can obtain fresh apricots, although I have made it with the canned variety and found it quite good.

	USA	Imperial	Metric
apricots	24	24	24
sugar	1 tbsp	1 tbsp	1 tbsp
flour	1 cup	4oz	100g
light brown sugar	½ cup	4oz	100g
ground almonds	1 cup	4oz	100g
butter or margarine	¾ cup	6oz	150g
blanched split almonds	½ cup	2oz	50g

If using fresh apricots peel and slice them. Arrange in a shallow ovenproof dish and sprinkle with 1 tbsp sugar. If canned apricots are used drain them well and arrange in dish, but omit the sugar.

Mix brown sugar, flour, butter or margarine and ground almonds together until mixture resembles coarse breadcrumbs. Spread over the fruit and stick the split almonds all over. Bake in a fairly hot oven (400° F, 200° C, Gas Mark 6) for about 30 min, until apricots are cooked and topping is lightly browned.

Eat hot with cream or custard.

Strawberries in Foil (serves 6)

A delicious dessert for a summer barbecue, when the foil-wrapped berries can be cooked over the fire, but they will cook just as well in the oven to be eaten indoors for an informal dinner party.

	USA	Imperial	Metric
strawberries	2lb	2lb	800g
castor sugar	¼ cup	4oz	100g
brandy	2 tbsp	2 tbsp	2 tbsp

Cut 6 squares of double foil, large enough to contain the berries—depending on their size. Wash and hull the berries and slice into a bowl. Sprinkle with sugar and stand for ½ hr. Divide berries and accumulated juice between the 6 foil squares, add 2 tsp brandy to each one and seal foil parcels well. Place on grill and cook over slow fire for 7–8 min, or put into a moderate oven (375° F, 190° C, Gas Mark 5) for about 8–10 min.

Serve hot over well-frozen ice cream or topped with well-chilled whipped cream.

Crème Brûlée (serves 4–6)

This is a classic recipe which for many years has been a speciality for dinner at the High Table at Trinity College, Cambridge. It is very rich and small servings are advisable.

	USA	Imperial	Metric
egg yolks	4	4	4
castor sugar	1 tbsp	1 tbsp	1 tbsp
double cream	2¼ cups	1 pint	568ml
salt	pinch	pinch	pinch
vanilla essence	¼ tsp	¼ tsp	¼ tsp
extra castor sugar			

Using an ovenproof dish which can be brought to the table, for serving, beat the egg yolks and sugar together until well mixed. Heat cream slightly and pour over eggs, stirring all the time. Add salt and vanilla and mix. Set ovenproof dish in a baking tin with 1in (2½cm) cold water and bake in moderate oven (350° F, 180° C, Gas Mark 4) for about 45 min, or until a knife inserted in the centre comes out clean. Chill well.

Just before serving sprinkle extra castor sugar evenly over the top to give a white surface. Put under a pre-heated grill just long enough for the sugar to melt and caramelise. Serve at once.

Baked Custard Brûlée (serves 4–5)

This is a family version of the above recipe.

	USA	Imperial	Metric
eggs	3	3	3
milk	2¼ cups	1 pint	568ml
castor sugar	1 tbsp	1 tbsp	1 tbsp
ground nutmeg	¼ tsp	¼ tsp	¼ tsp
salt	pinch	pinch	pinch
seedless raisins	3 tbsp	3 tbsp	3 tbsp
soft brown sugar, as required			

Pour boiling water over raisins, drain and dry well. Lightly beat eggs, castor sugar, nutmeg and salt together, then beat in milk and add raisins. Pour into ovenproof dish, and stand this in baking dish with 1in (2½cm) cold water and bake in moderate oven (350° F, 180° C, Gas Mark 4) for about 45 min, or until knife inserted in the centre comes out clean. Chill. Just before serving sprinkle a thick layer of soft brown sugar over the top, put under a hot grill until sugar has caramelised, but be careful it does not burn. Serve at once.

Cherries Jubilee (serves 6)

An elegant dessert to finish a special meal. Bring this to the table flaming ceremoniously, and if your dining room is lit only with candles it will look all the more spectacular.

	USA	Imperial	Metric
canned black cherries	2lb can	2lb can	800g can
blackcurrant jam	¼lb	¼lb	200g
brandy	¼ pint	4 fl oz	113ml
double cream	1¼ cups	½ pint	284ml

Drain cherries and place them in an ovenproof dish which can be brought to the table for serving. Spread the jam in an even layer over the cherries and heat in a moderate oven (350° F, 180° C, Gas Mark 4) for 10–15 min. Whip cream until stiff and chill for 15 min, then using an icing pipe, pipe the cream into 6 sweet dishes or glasses.

When ready to serve, take cherries from the oven and pour the warmed brandy over them, set it alight and carry the dish flaming to the table. It is then passed round for guests to help themselves into the prepared dishes.

One version of this recipe suggests that the cherry juice should be slightly thickened with a little arrowroot or cornflour, flavoured with some cherry brandy, and served in a separate sauce jug for guests to help themselves.

Kentish Cherry Cobbler (serves 6)

Kent is renowned for its cherries and apples, and this is a very old farmhouse recipe which can also be made with apples instead of cherries, if preferred.

	USA	Imperial	Metric
self-raising flour	2 cups	8oz	200g
sugar	2 tbsp	1oz	25g
butter or margarine	2 tbsp	2oz	50g
egg	1	1	1
milk, as required			
light brown sugar	1 tbsp	1 tbsp	1 tbsp
cherries, cooked or canned	2lb	2lb	800g

Sift together flour and sugar into a basin and rub in butter or margarine until like coarse breadcrumbs. Add egg and just enough milk to make a soft dough. Turn out on lightly floured board and knead lightly, then roll out and cut into rounds about ½in (1cm) thick. Turn cherries into a baking dish and heat well, then place rounds of dough on top, close together. Brush these over with milk and sprinkle with brown sugar. Bake in a fairly hot oven (425° F, 220° C, Gas Mark 7) for 8–10 min until risen and browned.

Serve at once, with custard or cream.

Baked Orange Pudding (serves 4-5)

	USA	Imperial	Metric
sugar	⅟₄ cup	4oz	100g
butter or margarine	⅟₄ cup	4oz	100g
eggs	3	3	3
self-raising flour	1 cup + 2 tbsp	5oz	125g
orange	1	1	1
orange marmalade	2 tbsp	2 tbsp	2 tbsp
castor sugar	⅟₄ cup	4oz	100g

Grate rind from orange, then squeeze out the juice. Cream together sugar and butter until light and fluffy. Separate yolks and whites from 2 eggs and put the whites to one side. Add yolks and the whole egg to creamed mixture with orange rind and juice, then fold in flour. Turn into a greased ovenproof dish and bake in a moderate oven (375° F, 190° C, Gas Mark 5) for about 30 min until well risen and firm. Spread top with orange marmalade. Whisk the egg whites until stiff, then fold in castor sugar until well mixed. Pile roughly over top of pudding and return to oven, with heat turned down a little, until meringue is set and golden. Serve at once.

Simple Baked Custard (serves 4-5)

This is quite the simplest pudding I know to make and it is always a favourite in our house, but I am always amazed at how many people have never made one.

	USA	Imperial	Metric
eggs	3	3	3
milk	2⅟₄ cups	1 pint	568ml
sugar	1 tbsp	1 tbsp	1 tbsp
salt	pinch	pinch	pinch
vanilla essence	⅟₄ tsp	⅟₄ tsp	⅟₄ tsp
seedless raisins	2-3 tbsp	2-3 tbsp	2-3 tbsp
ground nutmeg or cinnamon, to taste			

Pour boiling water over raisins and stand for a few minutes, then drain and dry well. Heat milk to luke-warm. Lightly beat eggs with sugar, salt and vanilla in an ovenproof dish. Add raisins and milk and mix lightly together. Sprinkle top with nutmeg or cinnamon. Stand dish in a baking dish with about 1in (2½cm) of water, and bake in a moderate oven (350° F, 180° C, Gas Mark 4) for 35–40 min. Test if custard is cooked by putting a dry knife in the middle, and it should be set right through.

Serve hot or cold.

Rice and Pear Meringue (serves 6)

This is a good dessert to make with canned foods from the cupboard when you are in a hurry.

	USA	Imperial	Metric
canned creamed rice	15¼oz	15¼oz	437½g
canned halved pears	15oz	15oz	425g
dark chocolate	2oz	2oz	50g
eggs	2	2	2
castor sugar	6 tbsp	3oz	75g

Separate egg yolks and whites and beat yolks into rice. Empty rice into ovenproof dish. Drain pears and arrange them hollow-side up on the rice. Grate chocolate and fill pear centres with the chocolate. Beat egg whites until stiff, then fold in sugar. Pile over pudding, covering right to the edge, and bake in a slow oven until meringue is crisp, about 20 min. Serve at once.

Rice and Peach Meringue

The same as above but use drained peach halves and fill centres with raspberry jam instead of the chocolate.

Chocolate Pear Upside-Down Pudding (serves 6)

This pudding is baked, then turned out with a design of fruit set in syrup on the top.

	USA	Imperial	Metric
Topping			
butter or margarine	3 tbsp	3 tbsp	3 tbsp
brown sugar	3 tbsp	3 tbsp	3 tbsp
lemon juice	1 tbsp	1 tbsp	1 tbsp
ground ginger	½ tsp	½ tsp	½ tsp
bottled cherries	6	6	6
canned pear halves	15oz	15oz	375g
Pudding			
self-raising flour	1 cup	4oz	100g
butter or margarine	4 tbsp	2oz	50g
sugar	¼ cup	2oz	50g
egg	1 large	1 large	1 large
milk	½ cup	4 fl oz	113ml
cocoa	2 tbsp	2 tbsp	2 tbsp

Prepare the topping first. Melt the butter or margarine in an 8in (20cm) sandwich tin and mix with brown sugar, ginger and lemon juice, spreading it evenly. Drain 6 pear halves and arrange, cut-side down on top of the sugar mixture, placing a cherry in the centre of each half (½ walnuts may be used in place of cherries if preferred).

For the pudding cream together butter or margarine and sugar until light and creamy. Beat in egg, then stir in flour and cocoa which have been sifted together, alternately with the milk. Beat until smooth, then pour over fruit in tin, being careful not to spoil the pattern. Bake in moderate oven (350° F, 180° C, Gas Mark 4) for 35 min. Remove from oven and stand for 3–4 min, then turn out on serving plate with glazed fruit on top. Serve hot with cream or custard.

Pineapple Upside-Down Pudding (serves 6)

Follow above recipe, but instead of pear halves use slices of canned pineapple cut in halves to make a pattern, and centre them with cherries. Omit the ground ginger in topping mixture.

The pineapple juice can be thickened with a little cornflour to make a sauce to serve with pudding if liked.

Fruit Roll in Syrup (serves 4–5)

A good old-fashioned pudding which makes a splendid ending for dinner on a cold winter's night.

	USA	Imperial	Metric
self-raising flour	2 cups	8oz	200g
salt	¼ tsp	¼ tsp	¼ tsp
castor sugar	1 tbsp	1 tbsp	1 tbsp
butter or margarine	2 tbsp	1oz	25g
egg	1	1	1
milk	3 tbsp	3 tbsp	3 tbsp
mixed dried fruit	2 cups	12oz	300g
extra butter	2 tsp	2 tsp	2 tsp
mixed spice	¼ tsp	¼ tsp	¼ tsp
granulated sugar	1 cup	8oz	200g
hot water	2 cups	¾ pint	426ml

Sift flour, castor sugar and salt together and rub butter or margarine into dry ingredients, using the finger tips. Make a well in the centre and add egg and milk beaten together, stirring in quickly and lightly to make a soft dough. Turn out on a lightly floured board and knead only enough to get a smooth dough. Roll out about ½in (1cm) thick into a rectangle 6in × 10in (15cm × 25cm). Soak the dried fruit in hot water for 10min, then drain and dry, and spread over the dough, leaving a 1in (2½cm) margin all round. Dot with the extra butter and sprinkle with spice, then roll up into a long roll and pinch edges together to seal firmly. Put granulated sugar and hot water into an oblong baking dish and cook over direct heat for about 5 min to form a syrup. Place roll in this syrup, baste well, and bake in hot oven (450° F, 230° C, Gas Mark 8) for 20–25 min, basting once during that time. Serve hot in slices with cream or custard.

Chopped dates, preserved cherries or chopped ginger can be added to mixed fruit if liked, or bottled prepared fruit mincemeat can be used for the filling.

Lemon Soufflé Pudding (serves 6)

A tasty pudding with its own built-in sauce which appears under a lemon sponge during cooking.

	USA	Imperial	Metric
butter	½ cup	4oz	100g
castor sugar	1½ cups	12oz	300g
eggs	4	4	4
self-raising flour	1 cup	4oz	100g
lemon juice	6 tbsp	6 tbsp	6 tbsp
lemon rind, grated	2 tbsp	2 tbsp	2 tbsp
milk	2½ cups	1 pint	568ml

Cream butter and sugar until smooth, beat in egg yolks, then stir in flour, lemon rind and juice and the milk and mix well. Whisk egg whites until stiff then fold into lemon mixture. Pour into a buttered ovenproof dish and place dish in a baking tin with 2in (5cm) hot water. Bake in a moderately hot oven (375° F, 190° C, Gas Mark 5) for about 1 hr or until pale golden on top. Serve hot.

Christmas Pudding

This is the Christmas pudding which has been a tradition in my family for many years. The amounts given here will make 3 puddings cooked in 2 pint (approx 1l) basins. They should be steamed for 7 or 8 hr on the day of making, then re-heated for about 1 hr on the day of serving.

	USA	Imperial	Metric
plain flour	2 cups	8oz	200g
mixed spice	2 tsp	2 tsp	2 tsp
ground nutmeg	2 tsp	2 tsp	2 tsp
salt	½ tsp	½ tsp	½ tsp
soft white breadcrumbs	4 cups	8oz	200g
beef suet	1lb	1lb	400g
seeded raisins	6 cups	1¼lb	600g
currants	2 cups	8oz	200g

CHRISTMAS PUDDING

	USA	Imperial	Metric
dates, stoned	½lb	8oz	200g
dried figs	½lb	8oz	200g
mixed peel	2 cups	8oz	200g
blanched almonds, chopped	1 cup	4oz	100g
sugar	1 cup	8oz	200g
eggs	6	6	6
milk	1¼ cups	½ pint	284ml
almond essence	1 tsp	1 tsp	1 tsp
brandy or rum	¼ pint	4 fl oz	113ml

Sift together the flour, spices and salt into a large bowl. Skin and shred the suet very finely (or use packaged suet) and mix with flour. Chop fruit finely, wash the peel to remove sugar if necessary. Soak fruit in the rum or brandy for some hours before adding to dry ingredients. Beat eggs and stir into mixture with the milk, then add essence and stir all well together.

Grease pudding basins well and two-thirds fill with mixture, cover with thick buttered paper or foil and tie securely. Stand on a rack in a big boiler or saucepan with enough water to come halfway up the sides of the basins and boil for 7–8 hr. Keep a kettle of water boiling to replenish the water as it boils away, and be sure water keeps on the boil. All this can be done some weeks before Christmas.

On Christmas Day, steam for 1 hr as directed above. Turn out and serve with whipped cream or hard sauce, made as follows:

	USA	Imperial	Metric
butter	½ cup	4oz	100g
castor sugar	1 cup	8oz	200g
brandy	2 tbsp	2 tbsp	2 tbsp

Cream butter and sugar together until light and frothy. Add brandy and blend well. Turn out on a flat plate and chill well until required. Cut in squares and serve 1 square to each serving of pudding.

Rum Hard Sauce: Make as above but add 2 tbsp grated orange rind and instead of brandy use half orange juice and half rum.

Flaming the Pudding: If you wish to serve your pudding flaming in the traditional manner you can use either brandy or rum.

Warm the spirit in a small saucepan, but do not allow it to boil. Place the pudding on a serving dish, then quickly pour the warm spirit over and around it and set it alight. But do be careful there is nothing inflammable near it which could also catch alight, and perhaps cause a fire.

PANCAKES

Pancakes feature in the everyday meals of many different nations under a variety of names. They can be served filled with a savoury mixture as the main course of a meal, or straight from the pan with lemon and sugar as a sweet.

They are very versatile, can be made in advance, stored in refrigerator or freezer, then when required can be filled with any one of a number of different mixtures and re-heated ready to serve.

To Store: Pancakes must be quite cold before wrapping for storage or they will be rubbery if re-heated. Cool quickly by placing pancakes on to a wire cooling tray after cooking. If storing in refrigerator wrap in foil or a polythene bag with the end tied and they will keep quite well for up to 5 or 6 days. To freeze, place rounds of oiled greaseproof paper or polythene between each pancake, piling them one on top of another. Wrap in heavy duty foil, and make sure all the air is expelled before sealing tightly. They will store in the freezer for 2 months. To thaw, leave unwrapped and spread out at room temperature for 20 min. Or leave, wrapped, in refrigerator overnight.

To Re-Heat: Pancakes wrapped in foil can be re-heated in a moderate oven (375° F, 190° C, Gas Mark 5) for 25–30 min. For filled pancakes with cold fillings, roll over filling, pack in a buttered ovenproof dish, cover with foil and re-heat in moderate oven for about 30 min, removing foil for last 2 min cooking time. If hot fillings are used with cold pancakes, they should be re-heated as above but only need about 15 min.

	USA	Imperial	Metric
plain flour	*1 cup*	*4oz*	*100g*
salt	*¼ tsp*	*¼ tsp*	*¼ tsp*
egg	*1*	*1*	*1*
milk	*1¼ cups*	*½ pint*	*284ml*
cooking oil, for frying			

Sift flour and salt into basin, make a hollow in the middle and break in the egg, then beat well. Gradually beat in half the milk to make a smooth batter, then beat in remainder. For sweet pancakes add sugar to taste.

If you have a blender the batter can be made by putting in the milk, then the egg and lastly the flour and salt, and sugar if using.

Add a little oil to the pan (I like to use a pastry brush) and heat until hot. Quickly pour in enough batter, about 3 tbsp, to thinly cover bottom of pan which should be tilted to cover bottom evenly. Cook until underside is golden brown, then toss or turn over with a spatula to brown other side. Repeat until all the batter is used up.

The number of pancakes which can be made from the above quantity of batter varies with the size of the pan used. I use my 7in (18cm) omelette pan, which is never used for anything other than omelettes and pancakes, and this gives 8 pancakes. A 5in (13cm) pan will give 12 pancakes, and a 6in (15½cm) pan gives 10 pancakes.

Pancake Gâteau (serves 6–8)

This can be made about 1 hr before serving time, wrapped in foil and put into a slow oven (300° F, 150° C, Gas Mark 2) to keep hot.

Pile hot pancakes up in alternate layers with sweetened stewed apples or apple purée, finishing with a pancake on top. Stand this on an ovenproof plate so it can come straight to the table from the oven. Other fruit can be used if preferred. Serve with cream.

Swiss Cherry Pancakes

These pancakes were served to me at a delightful hotel overlooking Lake Locarno, and even if you cannot get Swiss cherry jam make them with the nearest available equivalent—cherry pie filling is also excellent for these.

Use the Swiss black cherry jam as a filling for thin pancakes or crêpes, rolling them up and packing side by side in a shallow buttered ovenproof dish. Sprinkle with a little kirsch, dust with icing sugar and bake for 15 min in a slow oven (325° F, 170° C, Gas Mark 3). Serve with whipped cream.

Orange Cheese Pancakes (serves 4)

Mix grated rind and the juice of a large orange with ½lb (200g) cottage cheese, and add sugar to taste. Divide this mixture between 8 pancakes, roll up and pack into a buttered dish then re-heat. Dust with icing sugar before serving with whipped cream.

Sweet Sauces

Such ordinary desserts as plain ice cream or squares of sponge cake can be made into really glamorous endings to a meal by the addition of a good sauce or an attractive garnish.

Here you will find a variety of these to assist you in making 'plain Janes' into something special for any occasion.

Chocolate Lemon Sauce
This is delicious over chilled canned pear halves, or slice the pears and arrange as a filling for a packaged sponge flan case, then pour sauce over the top and chill before serving.

	USA	Imperial	Metric
canned cream	6oz can	6oz can	150g can
cocoa	2 tbsp	2 tbsp	2 tbsp
lemon juice	1 tbsp	1 tbsp	1 tbsp
castor sugar	1 tbsp	1 tbsp	1 tbsp
vanilla extract	½ tsp	½ tsp	½ tsp

Pour cream into a bowl and sprinkle with cocoa. Chill for 15 min.

Add lemon juice and beat until very thick, then add sugar and vanilla and beat until sugar is dissolved. Chill well.

If cream is too thick add a little top milk.

Instant Chocolate Sauce

Make this if you have an electric blender.

Put a 6oz packet of semi-sweet chocolate pieces into blender with 5 tbsp very hot water, hot milk or hot coffee as you please, cover and blend at high speed until smooth.

For a peppermint flavour use 6oz chocolate peppermint creams and 5 tbsp hot milk.

Raisins Jubilee Sauce (serves 4)

This becomes very special when it is flamed before pouring over well-frozen ice cream.

	USA	Imperial	Metric
seeded raisins	1 cup	4oz	100g
orange rind, grated	1 tsp	1 tsp	1 tsp
lemon rind, grated	½ tsp	½ tsp	½ tsp
orange juice	1 tbsp	1 tbsp	1 tbsp
lemon juice	1 tsp	1 tsp	1 tsp
brown sugar	2 tbsp	2 tbsp	2 tbsp
brandy	2 tbsp	2 tbsp	2 tbsp

Put raisins into bowl and cover with boiling water, stand for 5 min, then drain well and dry, Put back into bowl with grated orange and lemon rinds and juice, sugar and 1 tbsp brandy and stand for at least 1 hr.

When ready to serve add remainder of brandy and heat in a small saucepan. Have ice cream served in chilled dishes, take sauce to table and set it alight, then pour over ice cream while still flaming.

Cherry Brandy Sauce (serves 4–5)

Marvellous served boiling over well-frozen ice cream.

CHOCOLATE CUPS

	USA	Imperial	Metric
canned cherries	large can	large can	large can
cherry juice	scant ¾ cup	¼ pint	142ml
arrowroot or cornflour	2 tsp	2 tsp	2 tsp
water	4 tbsp	4 tbsp	4 tbsp
cherry brandy	4 tbsp	4 tbsp	4 tbsp

Blend arrowroot or cornflour with the water. Heat the cherry juice drained from the canned cherries, and stir in the arrowroot, stirring until the juice thickens and becomes clear. Stir in cherries and bring just to boiling point, then stir in cherry brandy. Serve at once over ice cream.

Apricot Brandy Sauce: Substitute sliced apricots or peaches for the cherries, and use apricot brandy instead of cherry brandy.

Orange Curaçao Sauce: Substitute orange segments, free of all white pith, for the cherries and use orange juice, 1 tsp grated orange rind and Orange Curaçao.

Pineapple Rum Sauce: Use pineapple juice, chopped pineapple and rum and follow above directions.

GARNISHES

Chocolate Cups (serves 8)

Fill these with ice cream.

	USA	Imperial	Metric
semi-sweet chocolate pieces	6oz	6oz	150g
butter	2 tbsp	2 tbsp	2 tbsp
foil patty-cake containers	8	8	8

Melt chocolate pieces and butter together over hot water, stirring until smooth. Cool to just warm. With a teaspoon swirl the chocolate round the inside of the patty-cake cups until the entire inside surface is covered with a thin layer of chocolate. Work quickly or the mixture will get too cool. Place the cups in a rack of patty-tins to keep their shape, then chill until the chocolate is set and hard.

206

When ready to serve, carefully tear away the foil, leaving chocolate cups ready to be filled with ice cream.

Frosted Grapes

These look most attractive as a garnish for ice cream or any fruit desserts.

Brush small clusters of grapes with beaten egg white. Toss them in castor sugar, making sure they are well coated, and leave to dry on greaseproof paper. Either purple or white grapes can be used for this.

Chocolate Raisin Clusters (makes 12)

Top a portion of plain ice cream with a cluster.

	USA	Imperial	Metric
dark chocolate pieces	4oz	4oz	100g
butter	2 tsp	2 tsp	2 tsp
seeded raisins	1 cup	4oz	100g
glacé cherries, halved	½ cup	2oz	50g

Melt chocolate pieces and butter in basin over hot water, stirring until smooth. Stir in raisins and cherries, stirring until well coated all over with chocolate. Put teaspoonful into paper cases or in small heaps on greaseproof paper and leave in a cool place until set.

Savoury Endings

The English seem to have been the only food-lovers (and they were indeed lovers of food from the eighteenth century onwards, when enormous meals were the order of the day) to have taken up the habit of eating a savoury dish after the pudding at the end of a meal.

The famous chef Auguste Escoffier thought it a deplorable habit and a gastronomical heresy, but fashionable hostesses still went on serving them, and many do so to this day. But today's hostess usually serves a savoury instead of a sweet, or serves a bowl of fruit as an alternative. The savoury usually takes the place of the cheese board, and many of these tasty dishes are made with cheese—as in the familiar Welsh Rarebit or Welsh Rabbit, whichever way you prefer to call it.

Many experts say that a true Welsh Rabbit must be made with beer, but one of the earliest versions, which is also perhaps the best, directs the cook to toast a slice of bread on both sides, then pour a glass of red wine over it and let it soak this up. Then cover it with thin slices of cheese and either toast it or put into the oven until the cheese is browned.

Simple Welsh Rabbit

Allow one slice of toast for each serving. The toast should be browned on both sides and placed in a shallow baking tin, then just enough brown ale poured over so it will be absorbed by the toast. Cover with slices of Cheshire or Double Gloucester cheese, spread a little made mustard over the top and either put under the grill or in a moderate oven until cheese is melted and lightly browned. Cut each slice into 3 and serve at once.

Welsh Rabbit with Beer (serves 2)

This is another old recipe for a traditional dish. Allow 1 tbsp beer with ½ cup (2oz, 50g) grated Cheshire cheese, and put into a saucepan with some pepper and some made mustard, stirring until the cheese is melted and smooth. Work in the beaten yolk of an egg at the last moment, then spread the mixture on fingers of toast. Serve at once.

Of course, for those who do not approve of alcohol, milk can be used instead of beer.

The only disadvantage to these simple recipes is that they really need somebody in the kitchen to make them and serve as soon as they are cooked.

Potted Cheese (serves 4–5)

This cheese mixture is made up 24 hr before serving, and is best if it can be put into small individual pots, and served with freshly made toast and pats of butter. Cheshire cheese is good for this.

	USA	Imperial	Metric
cheese, grated	1lb	1lb	400g
butter	4 tbsp	2oz	50g
sherry	½ cup	4 fl oz	113ml
cayenne, few grains			
mace	½ tsp	½ tsp	½ tsp
dry mustard	¼ tsp	¼ tsp	¼ tsp

Soften the butter without melting it, and beat all ingredients together until smooth. Or put through an electric blender. Press into small pots, cover with greaseproof paper or foil and chill for 24 hr, but bring back to room temperature before serving.

Herbed cheese can be made by adding chopped fresh herbs such as

O 209

parsley, sage, thyme and basil (about 2 tbsp altogether), and blending well.

Or make Bierkase by substituting beer for the sherry, and adding 1 tsp grated onion to the mixture.

Cheese Tartlets (makes 12)
Serve these hot and bubbly from the oven to finish off a good dinner, or they would make a tasty addition to a buffet party.

	USA	Imperial	Metric
shortcrust pastry (p 172)	8oz	8oz	200g
Cheddar cheese, grated	1 cup	4oz	100g
eggs	2	2	2
milk or single cream	2 tbsp	2 tbsp	2 tbsp
salt and pepper, to taste			
dry mustard	½ tsp	½ tsp	½ tsp

Roll out pastry and line 12 tartlet tins. Mix remainder of ingredients together and put a heaped tsp in each pastry-lined tin, and bake for 10 min in a fairly hot oven (400° F, 200° C, Gas Mark 6) then reduce heat to moderate for a further 5 min, or until pastry is cooked and filling just bubbling.

Cheese Tart
If preferred, use the pastry to line an 8in (20cm) pie plate, prick the bottom several times, then cover the base of pie with cheese sliced instead of grated. Beat eggs with milk and seasonings and pour over cheese, then bake as above. Swiss cheese such as Emmentaler can be used for a change.

Savoury Pancakes
These can be prepared ahead of time, then heated in the oven for about 10 min before serving. Make up required number of pancakes, allowing 2 or 3 for each serving—depending on how substantial the dinner has been already—and fill with a mixture of grated cheese, chopped toasted almonds and just enough cream to bind mixture together.

Season with a few grains of cayenne, and roll up firmly, packing the rolled pancakes into a shallow ovenproof dish. Add 2 tbsp cream over the top, then sprinkle with grated Parmesan cheese. Put into a moderately hot oven (375° F, 190° C, Gas Mark 5) until nicely browned on top. (See *p* 201.)

Another version of these is to fill the pancakes with cottage cheese, then roll them and cover top with grated Parmesan cheese. Bake as above.

Cheese Soufflé (serves 4)

Soufflés must always be taken straight from the oven to the table or they will fall like stones and go leathery—so don't attempt to serve one unless you have somebody in the kitchen to cook it and serve it at the right moment.

	USA	Imperial	Metric
butter	*2 tbsp*	*1oz*	*25g*
flour	*2 tbsp*	*½oz*	*12½g*
milk	*ample ¼ cup*	*¼ pint*	*142ml*
eggs	*3*	*3*	*3*
salt, to taste			
cayenne, few grains			
Cheddar cheese, grated	*1 cup*	*4oz*	*100g*
Worcestershire sauce	*1 tsp*	*1 tsp*	*1 tsp*

Melt butter and stir in flour, cooking for 1 min. Remove from heat and stir in milk gradually, return to heat and bring to the boil, stirring all the time, and cook for 1 min. Allow to cool slightly, then stir in egg yolks, seasonings and cheese. Whisk egg whites until stiff, add a spoonful to soften the mixture then fold in remainder. Pour into a buttered 6in (15cm) soufflé dish or casserole and bake in the middle of a moderately hot oven (375° F, 190° C, Gas Mark 5) for 25–30 min, or until well risen. Do not open oven door for first 15 min cooking time.

Fried Cheese Fingers

Use either Swiss Gruyère cheese or Danish Samsoe for these, which like so many of these savoury recipes, need somebody in the kitchen to do the cooking at the last minute.

Cut the cheese into fingers about ¾in (2cm) thick. Dip each one in beaten egg seasoned with salt and pepper, then into breadcrumbs. Let this coating dry, then repeat. Place on greaseproof paper and chill until ready to cook. They can be fried in butter in a frying pan, turning to brown evenly, or deep fried in hot oil until browned, then drained well. Serve at once, garnished with fried parsley sprigs.

Another version of this recipe dips the cheese fingers into batter before frying.

Short Guide to Cheese

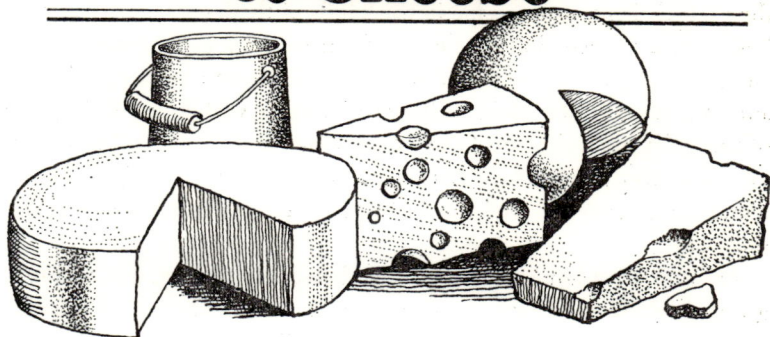

Many different lands claim to have discovered how to make cheese, and knowledge of this art has been part of legend and history going back to before the time of the Old Testament. And there are few civilised countries where cheese is not made today, giving us an amazing number of cheeses to choose from in our everyday diet.

But every country has its specialities, cheeses whose names we immediately associate with a country or perhaps a province or county, even though over the years those same cheeses have been copied in other countries—unfortunately, not always with success and sometimes to the detriment of the cheese.

English Cheddar is probably one of the best known, although today it is copied by the cheese-makers in many other countries. It has been made in the shadow of the Mendip Hills, close by towering Cheddar Gorge, since the sixteenth century, and is the 'prodigious cheese of delicate taste' of which William Camden wrote in Elizabethan times. Nowadays it is also made in Wiltshire, Dorset and other counties.

Older still is Cheshire, which has been known in the county of that name since the twelfth century. A mild and mellow cheese, sometimes richly coloured or creamy white, it also comes in a blue-veined variety. From Gloucester comes both Single and Double Gloucester, but very little single cheese (which refers to its size) is made today. A full-flavoured, mellow cheese, it should not be cut too young.

There are many others: gentle Caerphilly from Wales; Wensleydale, made by Cistercian monks until the Reformation, and when they fled they left their precious recipe in the hands of the local farmers' wives; Leicester, a russet-coloured cheese which makes a good contrast on a cheese board; Derby which is sometimes flavoured with sage leaves, and of course, Stilton, rich, mellow and creamy with blue veining, one of the really great cheeses of the world, which has only been known for just over 200 years. There are several stories about its origin, but its name came from the Bell Inn in Stilton, Leicestershire, where it was first sold.

Another very famous blue-veined cheese, Roquefort, has a history going back many centuries—legend says it was known in Roman times, but we do know that King Charles VI of France issued a decree in 1411 restricting the name Roquefort to the cheese made in the Roquefort district of the Causses in the caves of that area. And it is these caves that give the sheep's milk cheese its flavour, for all genuine Roquefort cheeses are ripened in the fantastic limestone caves of that area. Some experts say that no other cheese can surpass the flavour of a good Roquefort, just as others say Stilton is the best—it is all a matter of opinion. And it is good to remember when ordering blue-veined cheese that the prime months for these are between November and April.

There are other blue-veined cheeses, probably the most popular being Danish Blue, or Danablu as it is popularly known. This comes in foil-wrapped wedges and makes a good addition to a cheese board. One of the earliest of all veined cheeses is the Italian Gorgonzola, first made in the Po valley in the ninth century. Rich and creamy, its characteristic veining is more green than blue, and it has a flavour all its own.

Two other cheeses we must mention in connection with Italy are Bel Paese, a soft, creamy-coloured cheese which comes in a round chipboard box, showing a map of Italy, and which can be used in cooking as well as for eating; and the other is Parmesan, which is so well known as the accompaniment to all pasta dishes when grated. It is a marvellous cooking cheese, but few people know it is also an excellent table cheese when young and moist and freshly cut. For grating the cheese should be aged and hard, with a grainy texture, and it is always best if you can buy a piece and grate it yourself, rather than buy it already grated. A sprinkling of grated Parmesan can transform a simple dish into something special, and it is widely used in many dishes from soups to salads.

Apart from Roquefort, probably the best known of the French cheeses is Camembert, with Brie a very close second. Best eaten in its place of origin, Normandy, Camembert comes in small uncut rounds with a whitish crust flecked with gold. When fresh it should be plump and yielding when lightly pressed, and if it has a smell rather like ammonia—don't buy it, for it will be past its prime. If you are buying a Camembert, or a Brie, which is already cut, never choose one which has a hard, white cakey middle.

From Switzerland we get two famous cheeses which are entirely different to those described above, both of which are excellent for cooking as well as eating. These are Emmentaler, easily recognisable by its large holes, and Gruyère, with the smaller holes and slight flavour of walnuts. These two go well together either in a fondue or on a cheese board.

Two more familiar cheeses, Edam and Gouda, come from Holland, and are much liked by those who prefer a mild-tasting cheese. Edam comes in a ball shape, with a red coating, while Gouda comes in the conventional wheel, and has a yellow covering.

ACKNOWLEDGEMENTS

I would like to thank the following for their assistance in various ways during the time I was testing recipes and writing this book:

The National Dairy Council who assisted with the colour photograph for the cover, and Barry Markham who photographed it.

The Flour Advisory Bureau, Herring Industry Board, Lea & Perrins Cookery Service, Heinz Recipe Service and Eden Vale Dairy Products for black and white photographs.

Thorn Domestic Appliances for their invaluable Kenwood Chef mixer and blender; Prestige for their metricated scales and pressure cooker; Charles Kinloch for the wines used; Danish Food Services; Mattessons Meats Ltd; Creamola Puddings.

And all those people all over the world who so generously shared their treasured recipes with me.

Index

Numbers in italics indicate illustrations

Watermelon Delight, 145
Welsh Rabbit, 208
Welsh Rabbit with Beer, 209

White Sauce, 116

Yoghurt Dressing, 121
Yorkshire Brandy Snaps, 133